5.75

Other Al-Anon publications

Al-Anon Faces Alcoholism
Living With an Alcoholic
The Dilemma of the Alcoholic Marriage
One Day at a Time in Al-Anon
Alateen–Hope For Children of Alcoholics

AL-ANON'S FAVORITE FORUM EDITORIALS

Al-Anon Family Group
Headquarters, Inc.
NEW YORK
1980

Al-Anon's Favorite Forum Editorials
© Al-Anon Family Group Headquarters, Inc. 1970

All rights in this book are reserved. Excerpts may be reproduced with the written permission of the publisher at:

Post Office Box 182
Madison Square Station
New York, N.Y. 10010

Third Printing

Library of Congress Catalog Card No. 79-126349
ISBN-0-910034-22-2

Approved by
World Service Conference
Al-Anon Family Groups

Printed in the United States of America
by The Book Press, Brattleboro, Vt.

Foreword

TODAY'S FORUM began with Lois, drafting our first Newsletter on a yellow pad at the old Clearing House. The yellow pad had to rest on her knee because there was only one desk and a table. Never one to complain, she simply went ahead each month, writing all groups to tell them what had been accomplished or proposed.

Lois continued writing the Newsletter for over two years while work increased enormously. A part-time staff member was needed to supplement our wonderful volunteers and we were fortunate enough to get Henrietta from among them. She took over the Newsletter. But as work kept mushrooming, the combined job of Newsletter and the office work was just too much for one person.

Shortly before that I had taken a full-time job in the United Service Organizations' Division of the YWCA National Board and had found it necessary to limit my volunteer work. It had been a wrench to give up my days at the Clearing House, where for almost two years, I had been assigned to corresponding with individuals and groups. More rewarding and stimulating work would have been hard to find. When I went to USO I was unwilling to sever all ties so I clung to my Al-Anon Board of Trustees membership.

One evening in the spring of 1954 after work at USO, I arrived late at a Board meeting. Lois interrupted the discussion to tell me about Henrietta's difficulty and said that the Board had suggested I take over the Newsletter.

Without any hesitation or misgiving I lightheartedly agreed and have always been happy I did. Perhaps if I could have looked ahead and seen the growth of the undertaking I might have paused, at least for a moment. For the first eleven years I worked on it nights and weekends but since I retired from USO, I work at home, giving it practically full time.

The first issue of the Newsletter I edited was that of June, 1954. At the end of 1955, the first full year, 12,210 copies had been mailed in the 12-month period. It is interesting to note that in the single month of December, 1969, the figure almost equalled that of the whole year of 1955, or 11,659 copies. But back in 1954 none of us even dreamed of such growth.

Lois and I worked together that spring to plan a more comprehensive publication than just news of groups and the Clearing House. Somewhere along here the groups were polled and voted to call it the "Al-Anon Family Groups Forum." We decided to have a Step, a Tradition or a Slogan discussion in each issue and Lois suggested I write a monthly "inspirational" article.

That description has always made me a little self-conscious because I so frequently question how anyone who persisted in so many mistakes for so long a time, could inspire anyone. I readily appreciated that such helpful articles would add value, however, and agreed to try. Later it came to me how very right Lois was when she suggested I write such articles. Paul (I Cor. 1:27) said long ago, "God hath chosen the foolish things of the world to confound the wise . . . the weak things to confound the things which are mighty."

All the misdirected efforts to help my husband, the heartaches, the unhappiness and turmoil I had caused and fostered, all that was a costly investment in failure. But it became capital upon which I could draw to prevent others from persevering in similar mistakes. My failures enabled me to explain how our program really should be followed.

And so this book came into being. When Lois proposed to the Board that our 1970 Convention book be a collection of my FORUM articles, her working title was "The Best of Margaret." That name was enthusiastically hailed by many readers. But we since have thought better of attaching any Al-Anon's name to any official publication of our fellowship. That decision was made, not because it would break anonymity, which it would not, but because Al-Anon itself is, and should be, more important than any of its members.

So it is that "Al-Anon's Favorite Forum Editorials" comes to you now. My great love for Al-Anon and my appreciation of all that Al-Anon has meant to me, comes with it. Editing the FORUM all these years has been a privilege impossible to deserve or to describe. Countless numbers of you have added immensely to its helpfulness for without your contributions of letters, experiences and encouragement, the FORUM would never have grown to what it is today.

Thank you and bless you. My love to you all.

Margaret D., Editor

January 7, 1970

Contents

		Foreword	
1954	June	Our Bonus *We too had compulsions*	1
	July	Our Large Place *Al-Anon helps tear down walls*	2
	September	"Kindness in Another's Troubles Courage in Our Own" *Al-Anon program gives perspective*	3
	October	Knowing Ourselves *Pain is a price paid for better understanding*	5
	November	Real Members *Every member benefits when all participate*	6
	December	Our Children *Program helps us to help our children*	8
1955	February	Help From Going to Meetings *Program yields only what is put into it*	9
	March	Now Is The Time *Program pays off*	11
	April	Good and Bad Talks *Best talks are planned carefully*	12
	May	What Is Your Favorite Sin? *There's a remedy for all of them*	14
	June	Choice of Ruts *Practice the program happily*	15
	July	What Is Living For? *We seek courage and serenity*	16
	October	Our Slips Are Showing *The A-Anon program leads straight ahead*	17
	December	Christmas Stocking *A year's work is examined*	18

1956	January	Why I Believe in Family Groups	
		Sobriety does not end all problems	19
	February	God's Help	
		Heavy burdens can be borne with help	20
	March	God's Will	
		We learn and follow it through Al-Anon	21
	April	To the Newcomer	
		Alcoholic drinking does not negate love	22
	May	The Night I Felt Like God	
		I learned a lot from a thoughtless girl	23
	June	Family Group Needed	
		Acohol education helps many	24
	July	Loving Kindness	
		Our serenity helps others	25
	October	Easy Does It	
		Al-Anon can lift us from despair	26
	November	Live and Let Live	
		Tolerance brings understanding	27
	December	Christmas Wish	
		Al-Anon enables us to help others	28
1957	January	Values	
		How to choose the best	29
	February	The Enemy Within	
		Al-Anon helps to overcome fears	31
	July	Seeds of Today	
		Look fears in the eye	32
	August	Time, Strength and Opportunity	
		We learn to correct our errors	33
	September	Doing God's Work	
		Ordinary people worked the miracle for me	34
	November	Picture of a Resentment	
		How it was overcome	35
1958	February	Are You in Your Second Childhood?	
		Renew faith, hope and trust	36

	March	Growing in Stature *Make the program your own*	37
	April	Whose Story Do You Tell? *Describe what helped you*	38
	May	Good Talks *Spend time to prepare them*	39
	June	Living the Program *You should live it to give it*	40
	August	A Full Meal *Condition yourself for real help*	42
	September	Faith and Hope *Doubts and despair are handicaps*	43
	October	What Really Counts *Each has his own job*	44
	November	Knowing Ourselves *Self—our most important study*	45
	December	From Me to Me with Love *Al-Anon brings tranquil mind*	46
1959	January	Our Program Has Everything *Every help is available*	47
	February	An Invaluable Education *Learn about yourself*	48
	March	Failure Has Its Place *It can serve as challenge*	49
	April	Comparison Shopping *Are you doing your best?*	50
	May	Strength *Confidence is sure to come*	51
	June	Time to Think *Look for underlying good*	53
	July	There's Always a Last One *This slip may be the last*	54
	September	What We're Here For *Grow spiritually with Al-Anon*	55
	October	A Sourdough's Self Discipline *Live one day at a time*	56
	November	All Human Beings Make Mistakes *Learn to accept yourself and others*	57

1960	January	Counting Our Blessings *It's not bad to dwell on good*	58
	March	A Blast of Fresh Air *Fresh look brings answers*	59
	April	If We Choose *We can live without fear*	59
	May	Learning From Experience *We learn from others*	60
	August	A "Do It Yourself" Method For Al-Anon *Don't expect too much for too little*	61
	September	First Things First *What we learn in Al-Anon*	62
	November	Quality of Prayer *It's a learning process*	63
1961	February	Make Straight the Way *Al-Anon clears our roads*	64
	April	Al-Anon Has Answers *How to overcome anger*	65
	May	Squares and Grannys—In and Out of Al-Anon *Distractions cause mistakes*	66
	June	Who Can Carry the Message? *Twelfth Stepping takes effort*	67
	July	Who's A Failure? *No one needs to fail*	68
	August	The Glory of Al-Anon *There's something for everyone in it*	70
	September	Steps to Heaven *Perfection comes from practice*	71
	October	No Little Plans *Search for serenity*	72
	November	Arise and Walk *Put your house in order spiritually*	73
	December	Gifts of Al-Anon *Everyone should Twelfth Step*	74
1962	January	From Me, to You, with Love *Laughter is solvent for self-pity*	75

	February	Patience Is a Virtue—and a Goal *Learn to practice it*	76
	March	Look Around You *Everybody needs something bigger than himself*	77
	April	We Need Your Thought, Help and Prayers *Help Al-Anon to endure*	78
	May	Death and Taxes *Seek growth through challenge*	79
	June	Problems Make Progress *How to surmount growing pains*	80
	July	Words To Live By *Face your fears*	81
	September	Be Still And Know That I Am God *We make our own hells*	82
	October	Acceptance *Al-Anon's greatest gift*	83
	November	As A Man Thinketh *Change the things you can*	84
	December	Special Christmas Wishes *Help for those in distress*	85
1963	February	The Wonder of Al-Anon *Its appeals are broad*	86
	March	Each Day's Business *Do it today*	87
	April	Loving Kindness *Practice it daily*	88
	May	Sharing in Al-Anon *One talk can change a life*	89
	June	Looking at Lois *Faces reflect our attitudes*	91
	July	Wall or Bridge *Al-Anon helps us rejoin the world*	92
	August	Doors *Al-Anon helps unlock them*	93

	September	Al-Anon In Action *What your letter to the FORUM might do*	94
	October	Al-Anon Gold *Literature repays study*	95
	November	Fear Knocked at the Door—Faith Opened It *Face up to any fear*	96
	December	Vaya con Dios *Try walking with God*	97
1964	January	Today's the Day *Now is the time to begin*	98
	February	Try It Again *Never give up*	99
	March	Al-Anon's Second Wind *How to keep on practicing the program*	100
	April	"Nothing to Fear but Fear" *Give yourself a chance*	101
	May	Stop! Look! Listen! *Caution helps us to better lives*	103
	June	Do It Now *Lost opportunities*	104
	July	Understanding *Understanding brings acceptance*	105
	August	Why Are You in Al-Anon? *"Suggested" program works wonders*	106
	September	Don't Bury the Past Too Deep *Use it to make your future better*	108
	October	Something for You to Do *We needn't be perfect to help*	109
	November	The Al-Anon Mail Bag *Countless recoveries bring joy*	110
	December	What's Wrong with Pollyanna? *Let's be happy*	111
1965	January	Attitude of Gratitude *Everyone owes someone something*	112
	February	Be Generous with Your Past *Pride and fear handicap us*	113

	March	Time to Stand *All of us need occasional lifts*	*116*
	April	Testimonial to March's "Time to Stand" *I put preaching into practice*	*117*
	May	In the Presence of God *Time to be patient*	*119*
	June	"This Is the Day" *Good or bad, use it*	*120*
	July	Joy in Al-Anon *Al-Anon grows amazingly in twelve years*	*121*
	August	"Sermons in Stones" *"Bad" meeting was not wasted*	*122*
	September	A Bug's and a Bird's Eye View *Be patient with yourself*	*124*
	October	Alice and Al-Anon *Help comes from group's understanding*	*125*
	November	All That's Needed *No one is alone*	*127*
	December	Our Twenty-four Hour Program *Self-discipline in Al-Anon*	*128*
1966	January	The Person I'd Like To Be *Each of us is three persons*	*130*
	February	The Wisdom of the Serpent *Active problems can be borne*	*131*
	March	Looking for God *Gold is where you find it*	*132*
	April	Ripening or Rotting *Tragedy helps or hinders*	*133*
	May	A Twenty-four Hour Program *We need to work all of it*	*134*
	June	When Evil Triumphs *"Mrs. Al-Anon" makes group problem*	*135*
	July	Living by Glimpses *Live the program fully*	*137*
	September	The Up-Hill Road *Acceptance comes from realism*	*138*

	October	Do You Pass the Buck?	
		Repay your obligations	*139*
	November	Winnie the Pooh and Al-Anon	
		Al-Anon will get you	*140*
	December	Christmas Can Be Every Day	
		Study of literature brings happiness	*141*
1967	January	Value of a Wastebasket	
		Toss away misconceptions	*143*
	February	Enter to Learn—Go Forth to Teach	
		Live on a two-way street	*144*
	March	Tale of Two Frogs	
		Do the best you can	*146*
	April	Thoughts on Waste	
		Don't just skim Al-Anon literature	*147*
	May	Adding a Cubit to Our Stature	
		Free yourself from resentments	*148*
	June	Which Is in Control—You or Panic?	
		Facing fears brings solution	*149*
	July	Peace Within Ourselves	
		Get the right perspective	*151*
	August	Twelfth Step Warm-up	
		Don't expect instant success	*152*
	September	Bounty of Al-Anon	
		Program sheds light in unexpected places	*153*
	October	Mark Twain's Cat	
		Follow program persistently	*155*
	November	The Best Years of Our Lives	
		Time brings freedom and perspective	*156*
	December	Christmas and Al-Anon	
		Help, given and taken, makes Al-Anon work	*157*
1968	January	Where Does Twelfth Step Work End?	
		It is endless and endlessly satisfying	*158*
	February	Getting Fit to Live	
		Program works the miracle	*160*

	March	Putting Away Childish Things *One never graduates from Al-Anon*	*161*
	April	Thoughts on Stretching the Mind *Al-Anon showed me a better life*	*163*
	May	Look for a Long Time *Detached study shows real values*	*165*
	June	A Tranquilizer Highly Recommended *I saw where I was slipping*	*167*
	July	Don't Let It Throw You *Giving up usually leads to trouble*	*169*
	August	Through Other Eyes *Our only way to grow is to understand others*	*171*
	September	"When You Can't Do As You Would . . ." *Contentment is possible*	*173*
	October	What Do You Want? *Fear keeps us from knowing*	*174*
	November	One Day's FORUM Mail *It spreads a friendly world before us*	*176*
	December	Merry Christmas to Al-Anons and Alateens *You may never know what help you've given*	*178*
1969	January	Even the Desert Blooms *Occasional discouragement isn't all bad*	*180*
	February	Who Would Want To Be Infallible? *There's no shame in acknowledging being wrong*	*181*
	March	Always Tend to Your Own Knitting *Desperation disappeared with acceptance*	*183*
	April	Serenity: Our Greatest Safeguard *Emotional upsets let evil enter*	*185*
	May	No Problem Is Without a Solution *You just have to look for it*	*187*

	June	Use Al-Anon's Armor to Combat Useless Fear *Al-Anon's program brings freedom*	190
	July	Al-Anon's Program Enlightens the World *Twelfth Step work is endless*	191
	August	Al-Anon Is Not a Sometime Thing *Why long-timers stay in Al-Anon*	193
	September	Al-Anons Are Modern Alchemists *Wasted years are turned to gold*	196
	October	Speak to Newcomers in Their Own Language *Identification with others is our goal*	198
	November	Al-Anon's Program Comes to the Rescue *Al-Anon puts a stop to self-pity*	200
	December	We in Al-Anon Have Priceless Gifts to Give *Al-Anon help is a gift above rubies*	202
1970	January	Putting the Past to Work for Others *We can let it wreck or enrich us*	205
	February	Anger Can Be Friend Or Foe *Sometimes anger is on the side of angels*	207
1963	April	Serenity Prayer, Part I	208
	May	" " Part II	210
	June	" " Part III	211
	September	But for the Grace of God *Alcoholism is an accidental illness which might have struck us*	213
	November	Al-Anon's Three Important Days *Al-Anon program removes regret, gives guidance and hope*	214
	December	The Lord's Prayer *Contains many of the Twelve Steps*	215
1967	January	Listen and Learn *Learn to cope by careful attention*	216

	February	Easy Does It *Makes Al-Anon work smoothly*	217
	March	Let Go and Let God *—Goes hand in hand with acceptance of powerlessness*	218
	April	Think *Only way to find proper solutions*	219
	June	First Things First *Determining priorities restores order to daily life*	221
	July	Words to Live By *Success comes from never giving up*	222
	August	Keep an Open Mind *Best way to get best help*	223
	September	Live and Let Live *We need to do both*	224
	October	Who Said "This Is a Selfish Program"? *Program is personal rather than selfish*	226
	November	Discussion of "We Have No Dues or Fees" *Where support is needed and why*	227
1968		Discussion of the Twelve Steps *(Fifth Step—May 1966, Ninth Step —Sept. 1960)*	228
1969		Discussion of the Twelve Traditions	247
		Index of Subjects	269

Our Bonus

"LET EVERYONE SWEEP in front of his own door and the whole world will be clean."

That wasn't written about Family Groups and Al-Anons don't aim to clean up the entire world. Most of us came to grief just by trying to take in too much territory.

Either we tried running things with too high a hand, weighed ourselves down unnecessarily by assuming guilt for another's drinking, tried too hard to stop it, or we soothed our deeply hurt feelings with luxurious baths of self-pity. None of it was good.

In our own way, though not as obviously, we were just as excessive as our compulsive drinkers . . . indulgence in hot anger, violent reproach, neurotic frustrations. Our attempt to retreat from the world in order to avoid embarrassment or shame, was exactly as uncontrolled as our partners' drinking.

Whether we acknowledged it or not, ours was a disease too—a mental disorder we'd let ourselves fall into, just as our alcoholics knew they had a deadly disease yet continued to take chances with it.

But through the Twelve Steps, we are learning, or have learned, just to sweep our own doorways. The inventory we now take is our own; we can find enough when we honestly look for it, within ourselves, to keep us busy sweeping only our own dooryards. Over the years we have accumulated enough trash, enough grime and dinginess in an unhealthy aloofness from life, so that we need only concentrate on ourselves. That's our job and it's a big, challenging one.

With the Twelve Steps and the whole Program to use as our broom, we can make our dooryards immaculate. We can bring back sparkle to tired lives, restore hope to beaten creatures who so shortly before thought themselves better dead. We can live again as we were meant to live.

And, sweeping only before our own doors, we can reap the extra reward, share in the bonus of knowing that we are helping to make the whole world clean.

Our Large Place

"I called upon the Lord in distress. The Lord answered me, and set me in a large place." Psalm 118:5.

Like so many of us, did you begin life as a confident, outgoing person with a family which meant the world to you and a wide circle of friends, interested in everyone from the grocer to the paper boy?

And, over the years of living with a problem too great for you, did you gradually shut yourself away from your own family, friends, casual acquaintances and any contacts which could be avoided, no matter how flimsy the pretext?

That's what most of us did. We didn't quite realize just how we were narrowing our world until one day realization came that we had built a solid wall between ourselves and our family, our friends and anything and everything outside the tight shells in which we had encased ourselves. Our shells were closer and more confining than those of snapping turtles. Porcupines were soft, companionable pets compared with the bristling creatures we'd become.

For shorter or longer periods, we lived withdrawn. For most of us, the first AA contact pierced the wall but it was only breached, not demolished. The understanding instantly felt among other husbands or wives, faced with identical problems, gave us hope. But, as it should be, AA was designed for alcoholics; the help we got was indirect and only partial.

In our Al-Anon Family Groups, however, we find the complete help we so desperately need. The application of the program, while it is still the same program, is designed for us, the sober members of families damaged by alcohol. Here is our opportunity to discuss just how the Steps apply to us, how they are best interpreted for non-alcoholics and we are constantly reminded to practice this program "in all our affairs."

We come to the Family Group in great distress; we learn to call on the Higher Power as we understand that Power, and the immediate hope, release from tension, and the new aim and insight gained from meeting with other members, gives us the knowledge that indeed the Lord has answered us and has set us in a large place.

From the narrow, pressing walls we have built, we see the day when our alcoholics are again their true selves, instead of unhappy slaves to incomprehensible, compulsive drinking. And it isn't too long before we've torn down our walls ourselves, cast off our shells—even though for a few, their alcoholic mates may still persist in drinking.

Truly, we are in a large place, with understanding, hope and faith to keep us in it.

"Kindness in Another's Trouble,
  Courage in Our Own."

THE LITTLE-KNOWN Victorian poet, Adam L. Gordon who wrote those lines had about as checkered a career as any of us. Born in the Azores, educated at Oxford, he went to

Australia later and joined the Mounted Police. Then he became a member of the House of Assembly.

There's nothing now to show what made him write them. The most skillful amateur steeplechase rider of his day, perhaps a bad spill was responsible.

Most of us have had plenty of ups and downs, and it didn't take a steeplechase to throw us. We did that ourselves with a stupid answer to a tremendous problem. Retreat from life because of fear, self-pity and resentment, is not good for even normal living—how much worse it is, then, for us who live with alcoholics and the consequent distortions of family life.

Our entire Al-Anon Family Group philosophy is indicated, however briefly, in these two lines: kindness, which entails understanding and patience towards others in like circumstances; courage, for ourselves to acknowledge our helplessness, our inability to run our lives alone, much less to direct the lives of wives or husbands; courage to admit our dependence upon a Higher Power to take over the job at which we have failed. And above all, courage to call upon that Higher Power to direct us and to accept direction, however it is given us. We may not like the answer but we ask and obtain the courage to follow it.

In the beginning, when we are freshly stimulated and excited by new hope, release and inspiration, we frequently have a lot of both hope and courage, but before we sink ourselves deeply into the program, we sometimes have

> *Courage in another's troubles*
> *Kindness in our own.*

This marvelous Twelve Step blueprint for a way out of despair provides many directions we glibly accept and quickly pass on to something else without sufficient effort to put those directions to work. Where we fail to live the plan ourselves, where we meet setbacks or defeat, we accord ourselves a less rigid judgment than we give others: we failed because we were tired, because we have to "let go sometimes" and can't always be expected to show absolute control; it has to be our turn occasionally. Thus we excuse ourselves.

It is only by constant, intense study of the whole program that we get the order right again and attain the kindness toward others and the courage in ourselves. When we succeed at this, even though the alcoholic problem with which we live is still an active one, we are given courage to make our lives count; to live in order and decency and not in trembling fear; to hold our heads up, with the sure knowledge that help is at hand when we call upon it; that the Higher Power can, and will, stoop to lift us up, as high as we will let Him.

Knowing Ourselves

THIS MONTH'S STOPPER—"Knowing ourselves helps us to live better with others."—is particularly apt to this issue of the FORUM because it fits so well with the Fourth Step. The fact that it was written for a pamphlet on mental health gives it even more significance as it broadens the application, not just to us, but to anyone struggling with a big problem.

We all know dimly that progress comes only with dissatisfaction: man grew tired of living in a cave so he built himself a house; skins and furs were stiff and clumsy so he wove supple cloth for his attire; the spoken word was too difficult to be his only means of communication so he devised the alphabet and written messages.

Back of all these was dissatisfaction, discontent with present circumstances or actual pain. Little as we like to acknowledge it, we must realize that pain is a necessary part of our growth.

Children sometimes grow so quickly they have actual "growing pains," which are lightly dismissed by thoughtless persons. But they are not fun for the one enduring them. Neither is the pain of spiritual growth which also can be attained only through dissatisfaction, unhappiness and a wish to progress.

If we allow ourselves to remain dissatisfied and unhappy, discontented with our lives, to wallow in constant misery and complain endlessly, we waste our opportunity to grow in stature. Life without pain to overcome and spur us on would be static and sterile.

Through suffering, if we accept it as the good it is meant to be, we can grow, can achieve an understanding that success is not just in material things, in living a pleasant, happy life—nice and comfortable as that would be—but in overcoming our own defects of character, in suppressing our selfishness and in living for others rather than for ourselves only.

No one knows better than we the pain of living with an alcoholic problem. But we, who honestly try to practice all Twelve Steps in all our daily affairs, know also that pain is the price we pay for a better and deeper understanding, a richer and more meaningful life.

Real Members

SCARCELY IS THERE a meeting where someone doesn't say, "I used to give a lot of lip-service to the AA program but the Al-Anon Family Group helped me to begin living it."

Many of us recognized the program as a wonderful way of life but since it was labeled "The AA Program" we didn't apply it to ourselves.

Someone once wrote, "One may hold a truth, yet without inwardly possessing it. The formula which we accept will lie sterile in our minds if we do nothing to apply it to the reality which it is intended to serve." This is where we came in.

Most of the program lay sterile in our minds when we used it only to take our partner's inventory; when we admitted only that he was powerless over alcohol but kept feeling we could somehow control or manage his drinking; when we heard AA stories and pointed out their application to our alcoholic partners.

We did more harm than good, although we thought we were helping. We really added to a burden which already was crushing him. We probably even prolonged the excessive drinking, because that was his way of fighting back, just as a child who has been put in the wrong will fight against correction.

But when we applied the Steps and the Program to ourselves, when we finally accepted the fact that we also were powerless over alcohol, and that we needed the Higher Power to help us, that we were given this problem, perhaps, for our own spiritual growth, then and only then did we begin to share in its wonderful workings.

Another person said, "Years ago, we found that loyalty is born of interest and that interest is the child of participation. As long as people work for a cause, and weave something of themselves into the moving fabric, that cause has powerful and lasting friends."

It doesn't much matter if Family Groups have friends, unless those friends are the powerful and lasting kind who have woven something of themselves into their fabric. Family Groups need the kind of friends who work for the cause and it doesn't much matter whether that work is washing up cups after meetings or being willing to speak at other groups, or spending time and thought on newcomers. All jobs have to be done, not just by one or two "old timers" but by each member of the group.

When each of us does his share, all of us benefit from the participation. When all of us participate, each of us gets more out of the program.

Our Children

ARE YOUR CHILDREN being crippled by a parent's alcoholism? It is accepted now as a family disease and since a couple constitutes a family, their marriage suffers from the malady. But the suffering is greater where children complicate the situation.

It is harder to see loved ones suffer than to suffer oneself; it is hard to accept the fact we cannot and should not spare our children all pain. Only by letting them surmount small hurts do we prepare them to surmount greater hurts they cannot avoid. If we try to hide or disguise alcoholism by saying: "Mother has a headache" or "Father isn't well," we fool ourselves. Four words from a neighbor's child, "Your Dad's a drunk," quickly destroy the illusion we tried to create; they make the situation worse by shaking confidence still further.

Parents should learn all they can about the illness and as soon as children are old enough to understand something is abnormal in their homes, should explain as fully as possible what is wrong and what is being done, or can be done.

Parents can and should put away their own fears to

inspire hope in their children. Lois tells of the dark years of Bill's drinking which must have been very difficult for her parents to watch. Yet all through those years Lois's mother constantly told her she believed in Bill and knew he would stop. Although she died before this happened, her faith in Bill and her certainty of his eventual sobriety was of the greatest comfort to Lois and many times gave her courage to believe herself. That was before the miracle of AA.

If a grown woman can get such comfort and encouragement from inspiration like this, how much more do bewildered and unhappy children need it!

Now that we know what AA can do and has done, we must practice the program closely enough ourselves so that we can help our children by its teachings. The constant use of the Serenity Prayer is a great aid.

Most children are thrilled by the concept of AA and often want to live the program themselves. It is wise to encourage them in this. The Steps, vigilantly and courageously lived, will help us guide our children until the miracle works for us and them.

Help from Going to Meetings

HAVE YOU SOMETIMES thought the Al-Anon program was a bit theoretical, perhaps a mite too idealistic and impractical, and that you had not quite got the help you were seeking?

Some of us thought that in the beginning but fortunately we caught a glimpse of something—we didn't know what, maybe a feeling of warmth and fellowship which made us return again and again.

Then our eyes and ears really began to open. Usually the change came only after a number of meetings, and particularly one where a newcomer sought help. Generally speaking, new male Al-Anons come resentfully and female ones with tears and trembling. But both have the same story: "I've done everything I could to stop the drinking but it gets worse and worse. I can't take it any longer. It's driving me crazy."

When you smiled at the "I did everything I could to stop the drinking," (who knows better than we just what the tremendous understatement "did everything" covers?), perhaps you did not realize just how much the Al-Anon Group had already done for you. Probably the smile was a sort of Mona Lisa one, which stemmed from an honest recognition that such acts were futile trickery, just as we smile at a child pretending he is a grown-up because he's put on his father's hat. But you did smile!

No one can live a normal life without hope; thus if you follow the Al-Anon Family Group suggestion of facing up to your worst fears and looking them right in the eye, you are making progress, for you will see there is a way out. If you think things couldn't be worse, it is likely they'll be better soon because they seldom, if ever, remain the same.

You can free yourself from fear and attain tranquility by rooting out and recognizing just what you fear most. If it is fear that family and friends will learn of a partner's drinking, honest recollection will probably show you that long ago they must surely have recognized that for themselves. If it is fear that he'll lose a job, that fear can be faced and plans made. No matter what the fear is, none is as bad as the nameless ones which keep you churning in turmoil, without direction or hope.

Growth in Family Group philosophy is sometimes slow and unnoticed. It may take an outburst from a bewildered newcomer to show us we have progressed. But the fact that we can smile at our own mistakes proves we have been helped. How much more is available to us if we work at the program, if we study and practice the Steps, say the Serenity Prayer, read and try to understand the pamphlets!

It is very old stuff to say that you get out of something only as much as you put into it. But you'll be surprised at what you'll get if you put yourself into this program: it may be yourself you'll get back. But it will be a more generous, decent, tranquil self and one infinitely more easy for you to live with.

Now Is the Time

IF FAMILY GROUPS have any perfect saints, I have yet to meet one such marvel in my fairly wide experience over a period of years with a number of groups. Most of us quickly realize our goal is perfection. We try to approach it as closely as we can but we do not need to feel we have failed if we cannot quite achieve it.

In trying, we stretch ourselves spiritually. By trying to work all the Steps, the prayer and the slogans of our program, we come closer to what we would like to be than we'd have believed possible a few years ago.

That we sometimes fail is no cause for despair. It has been said, "Of all bad habits, despondency is among the least respectable," so when we do fail we pick ourselves up and immediately begin again. There is no going back to the pre-Group days when we reveled and sank in self-pity and resentment.

We have set ourselves this new goal of serenity and helpfulness to others. Many people feel that Lent is a time of preparation, atonement for past misdeeds and preparation for joy to come. Lent is here, and whatever our creed, now is a good time to concentrate deeply upon our aims.

Why not try working harder at whatever part of the program has been difficult? If it happens that you are diffident, pick out some member of the group and make a real effort at being friendly, or perhaps just listen attentively to a newcomer in trouble.

If your problem is one of acceptance, real work and thought on the Serenity Prayer will help. "Let Go and Let God" will take you a long way toward accepting any situation if you really put God first. Stop trying to run things alone.

Here's an idea: divide up the rest of Lent. After figuring out just where you need the most work on the different parts of the program, concentrate a certain portion of time on each place you wish to improve—a few days on the part where you have begun to improve and a couple of weeks on the toughest spots.

Good and Bad Talks

"I AM JOAN, married to an alcoholic for twenty years. We were happy at first until Ben began drinking. He went from bad to worse until he drank most of the time, practically never was sober. I got afraid to have the children near him. He was in the hospital four times and I began to think of leaving him . . ." Then follows a long, detailed account of perhaps fifteen years of plain and fancy drinking—all too familiar to all of us, winding up with a brief plug for AA and the Family Group in general terms.

How many times have you heard just such a talk, and

how much did it help you or the person making it? Mostly it was simply a tale of woe, better left untold.

Common experience and shared background is the foundation, the true backbone of the help we get from each other. But our talks differ from those of AAs, or should, and too many of us have patterned them after AA speeches.

There they qualify themselves as alcoholics by outlining detailed experience, how sick they were and what they did to get well. We need only say our partners are alcoholic to qualify us. Dwelling on it further wastes time better spent on the program itself, on specific instances of help.

Take me—I could say with truth that I had made myself ill with worry and thought I was losing my mind. That is true. But how much better if I say,

"Strain made me neurotic to the point where I associated changing the sheets on my husband's bed with his starting on a binge. To avoid starting one, I sometimes left them until they were gray and I was sick with shame.

"At the first Family Group meeting I attended, I heard a poised, happy young woman tell how she had done the same thing with her curtains. When she laughed at herself, I suddenly saw I wasn't going insane and went home to change my beds."

Nothing anyone has ever said since has helped me as much as that initial lifting of an intolerable load. And it was lifted because the instance was so specific. In dozens of talks since then, I have found countless others who had similar phobias and were equally hagridden by them. Each time I have told this, one or more of the group has told me of a similar superstition and of a new resolve to overcome it, as I had mine.

Not everyone is as lucky as I was at a first meeting but if you pick out some definite failing, some particular instance of your past and tell it, along with the things which helped you over the hump, you are bound to reach someone with experience so similar that he will be helped as dramatically as I was. What satisfaction is equal to that?

We say our program is to help us improve ourselves and our work is on ourselves. Let us study to see that there is where we do keep the emphasis, always. Our talks should be on what we were like, what helped us to change and, where we had difficulty in the program, how we overcame those difficulties.

There are few better means of getting the program than actually making talks at meetings. In order to give help to others, we must understand and practice the program ourselves. To prepare a really good talk we must sort out and re-evaluate the whole program and thus it becomes graven deeper on our minds.

Each of us is capable of either a good or a bad talk. The person who makes the kind first quoted is exactly as able to make a helpful one as the person who brings them up out of their chairs.

It takes only a little more thought, a little more time for sifting out ideas and selecting particular instances so someone "out there" will be at one with the speaker. Try it, soon!

What Is Your Favorite Sin?

THE OTHER DAY I came across a little pamphlet headed, "What Is Your Favorite Sin?" It startled me and I read on.

"Take your pick: do you think the first and worst is sex? What about murder, laziness, jealousy, over-indulgence, or anger, stealing, backbiting?"

I stopped and thought that perhaps my favorite sin was speaking too hastily, being too quick to criticize or comment sharply, but I read on: "These and all the rest have one thing in common. The root of them all is self-centeredness. And Christians believe that Sin in any form is putting yourself ahead of God. So—if your favorite sin is getting you down, don't worry. There is a remedy."

A moment's reflection showed me just how right the pamphlet was—all my failings do come from self-centeredness, although I seldom think of myself as selfish. But I have let worry get me out of balance.

I know now what the trouble is and how to fix it. And I don't believe it was coincidence that the pamphlet came my way while I was thinking especially of the Eleventh Step. I believe the Power Greater than myself was lighting my way.

Choice of Ruts

WHO SAYS ALL RUTS are bad? Somewhere in the North Woods there's a sign which reads "Choose your rut carefully; you'll be in it for the next twenty miles."

I've driven some bad roads, out in the high Rockies, but I've seldom seen one where you could not go at least ten miles an hour. So, even at that worm's pace, a bad rut lasted only two hours.

But what of us, closely tied to alcoholics? We know alcoholism is a permanent disease, which is arrested but never cured. That surely is a thing we cannot change.

It is true we can change the tie, but if we decide to remain with the sufferer—even for only one more week or day—we can change the way we spend that time.

Too many of us have spent years in the old rut of self-pity and resentment. We didn't call it that because those aren't pretty sentiments. It's easier to fool ourselves that we were concerned only about our loved one, more soothing to an already bruised ego.

But with courage and detachment, with the help of the program, we can see what an appalling rut we are, or were, in. Conscious and conscientious practice of all the principles of the program lifts us out of the old, bad rut into a good, healthy way of life in which we have courage to meet whatever comes.

If we choose this new rut we can stay in it, not for twenty but for all the miles that lie ahead, and we can make them happy miles.

What Is Living For?

IN A GRIPPING murder mystery a question, and a statement, jumped off the page at me: "Just what do you think living is for?" and then "The one unforgivable fault is weakness."

I tried to read on but forgot the thriller as realization grew that this question and intimated answer are a ready-made approach to our Family Group Program.

If you think your life is for pleasure, distraction or limited to your own self, then probably you'll never read this article nor be in an Al-Anon Group, because we believe life is for growth, both mental and spiritual.

That growth began, for most of us, when we accepted the fact that compulsive drinking wasn't a weakness but the result of a disease. We grew a little more when we looked within ourselves and found weakness there—weakness in the way we had refused to meet our problem, in the way we had attributed all fault to the alcoholic and in prolonged self-pity.

The Steps for us have been steps up to a higher plane. From them we have learned we are less than perfect ourselves and likely to remain so but that, following the Steps, we can gain courage and serenity to make our lives count toward good and not add to the evil already in the world.

We can become helpers, not helped; givers, not takers. Gradually we leave weakness behind us and learn that growth, although painful, is worth the suffering.

Just what do *you* think living is for?

Our Slips Are Showing

WHEN I TOOK a half-slip from a drawer my husband asked what it was. "They used to be petticoats but now they're half-slips," I answered.

"Half-slips are something AAs can't have," he said and I quickly agreed. And the quip stuck in my mind: I decided that while AAs can't have half-slips, Family Groupers can—and sometimes do.

If we have spent even a short time only in conscientiously following our program, trying to live the Steps to the fullest, we are not likely to fall back completely into the old, bad ways.

But every time we worry about next month, or say a quick and cutting thing to someone or let personal prejudice distort our thinking, we are indulging in a half-slip.

And half-slips turn into real slips if we persist in them.

Christmas Stocking

EVERYONE LOVES TO WATCH a child pull treasures from his Christmas stocking. The rubber ball, bubble pipe, spacegun or tiny doll are ordinary enough toys but to the child, each is a separate surprise and enchantment.

If our Family Group contribution could be wrapped in tangible form and put in our Christmas stockings, I wonder if we'd be happy to view a year's work in a field where such marvelous opportunities are given to each of us.

Would we open up package after package of friends and strangers made happier by the time, effort and thought given to them by us at moments when they desperately needed comfort and hope? Would we find unexpected little what-nots, tucked in here and there, which represented thoughtful comments at meetings? Would we find a shining star which meant we had met every challenge—or even just most of them?

I know the temptation of letting some one else take on the new person at meetings and no one knows better that it's hard to contribute when you're tired: no idea seems worth putting into words. But perhaps that's your unique opportunity to reach someone else by telling of the very thing which disheartened you.

"To whom much is given, much is expected" may sound like old stuff but it's old because it's good. We have been given much in this program of ours and I hope all of you find much to enchant you in this make-believe Christmas stocking. May you all find pride in the hope, help and joy you have given others.

Why I Believe in Family Groups

AT THE St. Louis Convention last July, someone asked me why, when her husband was successfully sober in AA for six years, she needed a Family Group?

I thought a moment and said AA was then celebrating its 20th Birthday and after all those years of Bill's sobriety, Lois still found help in Al-Anon Family Group work and in living our program. Undoubtedly there was a better answer but I couldn't think of one at the time.

Right now I can't speak of any such period of sustained sobriety. But knowing myself, I believe if there were years of it behind us, I still would need to keep close contact with this work. Without the numerous eye-openers every meeting affords, without the constant jabs which come from realizing another's courage when my own is failing, without the many sidelights on how to meet and overcome difficulties which each talk gives, I'm sure I would, sooner or later, slip back into my old complacency. And what is more disgusting than complacency?

This program, properly lived, first helps us meet the problem of living with alcoholism. It doesn't stop there or it isn't being lived properly. It is a program of spiritual growth, one which helps us meet every other problem life brings. It has already helped me with the first problem and with others not connected with alcoholism.

When the day comes that I can say there's been a year, or six or ten, of sobriety in our home, I'll be saying it at a Family Group meeting, because there's where I keep finding the way to living as I like to live.

God's Help

A GREAT PART of our Family Group program, like its parent AA, is spiritual. Some people have difficulty in accepting that spirituality. They approach it as a reluctant swimmer risks one toe in a cold sea.

For the most part, I plunged wholeheartedly into the spiritual thinking. What bothered me was the practical side, the recognition that I was powerless over alcohol.

One troublesome thought, however, kept popping up to distract me from complete spiritual serenity: when things were bad, I'd comfort myself by remembering God's promise that He never would give me a burden too heavy for me to bear. And I'd say a prayer and feel better.

But sometimes the thought would stray across my mind, "What of those people who commit suicide, or go insane? Their burdens *must* have been too heavy for them." Then I'd pray some more and the nagging doubt would go, although a shadow of it remained to trouble me.

Since this is my own particular corner of the FORUM, and I've never pretended to be wise, I can admit here that it wasn't too long ago that, suddenly, the answer to this question flashed into my mind. Now it seems incredible that I ever was bothered about it or that I should have been so long in finding the answer.

It's such a simple one: the burden will never be too great *if* you ask God's help in bearing it and if you *earn* that help by following His Will.

God's Will

HAVE YOU EVER been troubled, wondering just what is God's will?

We say in the Third Step that we "turn our will and our lives over to the care of God as we understand Him," which means that we'll try to live according to His will. More specifically, in the Eleventh Step we "pray only for knowledge of His will for us and the power to carry that out."

But what is God's will?

He seldom speaks directly to us, although He has done so in the past. We still live in this world, and there are decisions which must be made. We can't sit back passively and wait for a flaming sword to direct our paths.

A lot of the time decisions aren't very important. Whether we walk to a given place or take the car can't matter much to God. But where issues and futures and serious things are at stake, how can we be sure we are following God's will and not just our own in a subconscious way?

That used to bother me, as it did my husband. But we have found the answer—a sure way to make certain it is God's will and not ours. Like so many other important things, it's a very simple way:

All that's necessary for us is to do *everything* we do *in* God's name and *for* God. Then we can't go wrong.

To the Newcomer

TO MANY OF US, the most difficult thing about a partner's drinking was the persistent thought, "If he really loved me, he wouldn't drink that way."

At first we didn't know a compulsive disease was responsible but even when we learned alcoholism is now accepted as the fourth largest health problem, the nagging sense of being rejected still was present.

Steinbeck says, in *East of Eden*, "I think everyone in the world to a large or small extent, has felt rejection. And with rejection comes anger, and with anger some kind of crime in revenge for the rejection, and with the crime guilt—and there is the story of mankind. I think that if rejection could be amputated, the human would not be what he is . . . one child, refused the love he craves, kicks the cat and hides his secret guilt; and another steals so that money will make him loved; and a third conquers the world—and always the guilt and revenge and more guilt."

I don't suppose many of us went around kicking cats or stealing but most of us in our own devious ways, did things in frustrated anger we were ashamed of. If *he* didn't love us enough to be sober, *we'd* show him it didn't matter. Rejection, pure and simple: a childish game of tit for tat. But we're now too old for such games.

Al-Anon Family Groups sooner or later teach us that alcoholic drinking is not a deliberate reflection of indifference, that it has nothing to do with love. When we reach this haven of comprehension, we are freed of the sense of rejection, of guilt and of anger we have fostered so long.

We have time and spirit, once we stop fighting ourselves, to develop an understanding, a sympathy and a serenity that makes our homes pleasanter places for all.

The Night I Felt Like God

COLLEGE SOPHOMORES are noted for thinking they know everything and apparently I was no exception because, as one, I caught a glimpse of what God frequently must feel when He considers mankind and its mistakes. It seems appropriate this month, when we are reflecting on the Eleventh Step, to recall that feeling and the help it has brought me all these long years.

I was in charge of costumes for the Annual Follies, a job much too big for me and one never before given a sophomore. I worked incredibly hard, especially on costumes for eight fireflies. We even used chiffon instead of paper cambric, so you can see it was the high point of the production.

Delicate, fairy-like, red-haired girls were chosen for the dance. I stayed with them until I saw they were all ready for their entrance. Then I went up to a vantage point, high in the wings, where I could look down and gloat.

Poor things—the flooring between their dressing room and the stage was cold and splintery to bare feet, so they slipped into flapping galoshes for the run to the stage.

Seven lovely sprites, all orange and flame, leaped to center stage and danced about a flickering fire. The eighth clunked along, complete with galoshes!

Into my head, without a pause, jumped the thought: "This must be the way God feels when we do something wrong. *He's* done everything but, given free will, *we* mess up all His work."

Many times since that night, fortunately before I've leaped, complete with galoshes, I've remembered that sorrowful moment for something lovely marred by thoughtlessness. And I've kept myself from messing up His plans for me.

I haven't always been successful but at least I caught a glimpse of what being really close to Him could mean and I've tried to get closer still.

Family Group Needed

A RECENT LETTER, signed but with no address, gave me great distress and concern. It was extremely vehement and I wish space permitted giving it in full. She wrote:

"Of all the tommyrot ever started, it's that people (the so-called alcoholics) are sick. They are no more sick than one who indulges in any other vice or is a glutton of any kind. A customer, a woman who goes on binges, came into my place and said:

" 'I am sick; I need treatment. I'm an alcoholic.' I said, 'There's no such thing. God did not make anyone a slave to any vice—you want to drink.' 'Yes,' she answered, 'it helps me to forget.'

". . . telling people they are sick only gives them an excuse to drink. To break any habit takes only determination and prayer. They're sick? My eye!"

Eventually ignorance such as this, I know, will be eradicated: with AA, the Al-Anon groups and the National Committee on Alcoholism all working to educate the world on this problem, it won't be many years before such a point of view is as outdated as the idea that the world is flat.

After all, it isn't too many years since mental illness was considered a disgrace, hidden because of shame, and mentally ill persons many times were treated less well than animals. Education in the field of alcoholism will surely accomplish as much for alcoholics.

But what concerned and bothered me most was the antagonism displayed—the ill-will shown. It worries me because I feel the author needs Family Group help. She sounds sick and hurt and fearful herself, and there's no way to reach her at present.

Since she was interested enough to write Al-Anon, perhaps she would be interested enough to go to an Al-Anon meeting in her home town sometime and we'll have a chance to help her.

Loving Kindness

SCRIPTURE TELLS US that even "a cup of cold water, given in My Name," will be rewarded. In Family Groups we are more likely to offer a cup of hot coffee with simple human kindness but the spirit is exactly the same, because whatever we offer is given through love and understanding. Our reward usually is immediate.

When we have attained serenity through practicing the Twelve Steps, it is so apparent to the disheartened newcomer or to the older member going through a difficult period, that each is reassured. Each knows he, too, can reach the same goal by embracing the program or by digging in deeper to recapture it.

Our own lives still may be troubled with the same old problem but we have learned, or are learning, to live peacefully with it. We may have other new and serious difficulties but we are learning to accept them with fortitude and the sure knowledge that they can be surmounted.

Gaining serenity is hard; holding fast to it frequently is difficult, too, but, in the main, we're grasping some of it.

Those troubled spirits who come to us in their despair

can sense our serenity. When they learn that our story, our life experience, duplicates their own, they get a strong ray of hope that their lives can and will be brighter, their burden lighter.

To help them look up with hopefulness, to show them they can gain that same serenity, to know they no longer live in despair—that is our immediate reward. And what a reward for just a simple, human kindness!

Easy Does It

IN YOUNGER and sillier days, my sister and I once charged up a Colorado mountain at the same fast pace we walked Chicago's flat streets. We did for a few hundred feet, that is. We then stopped, gasping for breath until our hearts stopped pounding like pile-drivers. We resumed at a sensible rate and made our goal.

Sometimes people try to swallow the Al-Anon Family Group program as heedlessly as we ignored altitude. A sort of mental indigestion is the usual result because this program is solid meat—not a quick lunch designed for four rapid gulps.

Most of us are too upset and too wrapped up in personal worries when we come into the group to be ready immediately for the Twelve Steps. Those take time and thought and plenty of reflection on what our true aim and goals are. Acceptance of them comes when we relax and lean on a Higher Power, not when we frantically tread a squirrel cage of activity.

Beginning in childhood, with fairy tales and legends, like the Hare and the Tortoise, Bruce and the Spider, and a dozen others, we constantly are cautioned to go slowly and steadily, to accept defeat and make another valiant try. That holds good for Family Group work—Easy Does It, but *do* it, and *keep on doing it.*

Bits of the program sometimes come easily and at once. Other times we seem to have it all in our grasp and following it is simple. We are lifted up and float through the days.

Then, perhaps because we have slackened our efforts, a day comes when we fall into old habits again and we feel we have failed. That is the day to take stock, to see where we went wrong and how we can put things right.

By now, too many persons have been lifted from despair by this program for any of us to have any serious doubt of its effectiveness. What we need is to follow it closely and steadily: it will work for all of us if we let it.

Live and Let Live

IN OUR MEETINGS we hear and speak a lot about tolerance. The dictionary definition of it is, "the disposition to be patient and fair toward those whose opinions or practices differ from one's own."

That's a good beginning, to my way of thinking, but it's just the first step toward true tolerance. Certainly if we close our minds to everything with which we do not agree, if we deny others the right to think differently, if we never examine our beliefs to see if, perhaps, we can widen our horizons, we ought to be cabbages, planted in neat rows in a truck garden, rather than valued members of such groups as Al-Anon. Cabbages have their place but also they have their limitations.

What we seek in Al-Anon is continuous growth, mental

and spiritual. We cannot achieve this growth unless we seek to enlarge our comprehension, not only of our principles but of people. And we cannot attain this comprehension without a concentrated effort toward understanding.

The French have a saying that to understand all is to forgive all. While differing from ourselves is not in itself a matter for forgiveness, once we understand another person thoroughly, we are more in sympathy with him. We accept the differences between us—frequently we grow in stature by this acceptance.

Learning to accept less-than-perfection in other people is, however, sometimes child's play when compared with accepting it in ourselves. Yet if we are to Live and Let Live, it seems to me that we should number ourselves among those who should be accepted. Many of us can readily understand failure in others but still make ourselves miserable over our own failures. Frustration and pressure build up in us because we fall short of our aim and cannot understand why.

Instead of aiming at instant perfection, if we were to choose one failing and work toward overcoming it, we would eventually succeed. We then could attack the next. Even if each effort took a year, it wouldn't be too long before most faults were much improved.

So, let's remember that tolerance is understanding—of ourselves as well as of others.

Christmas Wish

FROM THE TIME when the Three Wise Men, bearing gifts, first followed the star to Bethlehem, Christmas has been a time of giving. We would find it difficult today, to make gifts of gold, frankincense or myrrh, and indeed, after the ravages of years, any gift at all sometimes seems beyond our power to manage.

But we do have gifts, those given us and those to give others, no matter how bankrupt we seem—the gift of gratitude that we have been led to Al-Anon, and the God-given opportunity we have there to help others; the gift of hope we have attained, which has strengthened us to attend another's dire need; the gift of serenity which has helped us and steadied our families as well.

But above these, the greatest gift of all is within each one's power, and that is the great gift of prayer. We've been led to believe again, or more strongly than ever before, in the Higher Power. We can pray that every person still in need of the precious gifts we have been given, will be guided our way and given them, too.

My Christmas wish is that I, and all of you, will always be grateful for these gifts, and above all, will be fervent in our prayers for others. God bless Al-Anon and all its members—a true Christmas to all of us.

Values

EVEN FOR SO SIMPLE a visit as an overnight stay, we plan our luggage and what we'll pack. How, then, shall we plan, with a bright New Year ahead? It will come only a day at a time but there's a year of days in which to accomplish our aim.

"What is life but a choice of values? We never lose anything by leaving it behind—we take it along in another form." Those are good words to remember in mapping out a new year.

Al-Anon has changed many forms for many of us.

Through it, we have learned that the shame we formerly suffered has changed to sympathy for another's illness. We have learned that anger and frustration can change to understanding and tranquility. We have learned that what we thought a curse has led us to our deepest happiness. Nothing has changed but our own selves, when we worked toward changing ourselves.

Once we recognize that our time, energies and capabilities are limited, we increase our chances for satisfaction by choosing to work on something within our scope.

For instance, I always wanted a lovely singing voice—that, to me, was the ultimate gift. As a child I sang constantly but gradually learned (from others; I sounded fine to me) that even with two baskets and a boy to help, I could never carry a tune.

I was unhappy over this until it came to me that if I worked hard enough at it, I might learn to make words sing for me and perhaps, through them, help another. No work would have changed my inability to sing but work *has* helped me to write.

Thus, in the year ahead, we can take along with us, in the best form possible, all that we have experienced this far. If we are still resentful, we can seek out something to replace that resentment, something which will help us and others too; if we are discouraged, we can aim at a year of hope and faith.

By concentrating on love and understanding, we can forget ourselves and lose ourselves in this most wonderful program.

Let's choose our values for 1957 carefully, and a Happy New Year to all in doing it.

The Enemy Within

WE ALL KNOW the parable of the householder who sowed his fields and whose servant came to him saying, "Master, did you not sow good seed? How then are there weeds in thy fields?" and the reply was, "An enemy hath done this thing."

We are like that man: we began with good seed—hope, faith and confidence that we could keep our lives strong and straight, but then the enemy came and we succumbed to doubt, fear and despair.

What we did not realize was that the enemy was within us, our human failure to cope with our own problems. Our excuse and explanation was a ready one: if we had not had to struggle with alcoholism, we'd have remained strong and sure.

In Al-Anon we have learned it is possible to live with this problem and return to our first surety of hope and faith. We have seen this happen to hundreds around us; once we accept the fact that our problems are separate from those of the alcoholic, a Higher Power leads us to the solution of our own.

As alcoholism is a progressive disease, so is that of our own neuroses: as long as we allow ourselves to wallow in self-pity and despair, as long as we distractedly run about trying to manage another's life, just that long are we letting the enemy within us stifle our power to climb into a haven of hope and serenity.

Once we truly admit we have *let ourselves* slip into despair because of something out of our control, we gain the first victory over that enemy. When we rely upon the Higher Power for help to rise from the pit we have dug ouselves, we get that help in abundance.

In Al-Anon we can see that others have obtained the strength they need and are living lives of faith and peace. When we gain this serenity for ourselves, it spreads to others—to our children and our families, and even to the alcoholic who needs it so terribly.

Recognition of the enemy within ourselves is our first step. After that the Higher Power will help us to go forward to live with restored hope, faith and tranquility.

Seeds of Today

"ALL THE FLOWERS of all the tomorrows are in the seeds of today." I ran across that recently when I was feeling about as hopeless as it's possible to feel.

Without realizing it, I had allowed myself to slip back into negative thinking where I looked forward only to more of what was making me unhappy. Suddenly I realized that if I continued as I was, those tomorrows *would* be grim and black—but they needn't be: Al-Anon had taught me different ways.

Al-Anon seeds, planted over the years, sprouted right then, anew.

First to pop up was the fact that I was not facing years of anxiety but only the one, present moment and it was gone while I thought of it—nothing had happened in it, either, except for good.

I made myself look back at other times and realized I'd managed to live through them, so likely I'd live through this. I sorted out my worst fears and looked them straight in the eye—individually, they didn't seem as bad as the mountain of evil I'd made them into.

Had I continued my merry-go-round of worry, I'd have

been ill—my present days would still have been full of the weeds of despair and heartbreak. But Al-Anon teaching pulled me up by my bootstraps so that today hope and courage are at my command.

Time, Strength and Opportunity

"Grant me strength, time and opportunity always to correct what I have acquired, always to extend its domain; for knowledge is immense and the spirit of man can extend infinitely to enrich itself daily with new requirements. Today he can discover his errors of yesterday and tomorrow he may obtain a new light on what he thinks himself sure of today."

Much as these lines sound as if quoted from a talk to Al-Anon members, they really are taken from the oath and prayer of a Jewish physician, over eight hundred years ago.

More than most people, we who have lived with an alcoholic problem, have acquired habits and traits which need correction. Time was when we knew no better but even a short while in Al-Anon has shown us that most of the things we formerly did were actually as harmful to ourselves as to the alcoholic.

So, strength, time and opportunity to correct these failures are needed by each of us.

As we learn, through our program, to accept alcoholism as a disease and the alcoholic as a sick person, we learn also how to condition our own response to the situation. Anger, fear, resentment and self-pity were doubly harmful weapons against it; most times they made that bad situation virtually impossible.

But as we have enriched ourselves through knowledge

and understanding, we have extended our horizons so that we can better recognize and cope with our problems. We require more of ourselves than an immediate, self-indulgent response to disagreeable circumstances.

By the new light we quickly attain in Al-Anon, we can correct our errors of yesterday. By diligent application of our Steps and Traditions, we can gain further light, because ours is a program of endless growth, with limitless possibilities.

Doing God's Work

READING ALBERT C. CLIFFE's "Let Go and Let God" (not, so far as I know, connected with AA), I came upon these lines concerning the power of prayer:

> *"Don't expect an angel suddenly to appear in person, but know and believe with all your heart that God works through ordinary folk like you and me, and that it is through ordinary people that good will come to you."*

Suddenly it came to me how right and how natural it is that help should come to us that way. Indeed, how else could we expect it to come? Since we are all children of God, He is in all of us, whether or not we are conscious of it.

I always prayed for help with the drinking problem in our home. But I prayed specifically for a miracle: a flaming sword suddenly thrust between my husband and a drink, scaring him green, so that he'd never touch another drop—something like that would have satisfied me completely.

Sometimes such spectacular visions do happen; they didn't in our case, but a quite ordinary miracle did and I got the help I needed so urgently. It came from the very people around me—exactly the ones I had long been trying to avoid, through shame and ignorance.

Through my fellow Al-Anon members I learned that alcoholism definitely is a disease, not a character defect. I learned that but for the Grace of God, I too, might have been a victim of alcoholism—with more difficult problems and a stiffer personal fight for control than that of the wife of a sufferer.

I learned that any one could contract this disease, just as unaccountably as one could be afflicted with heart trouble, arthritis or cancer.

With the realization that my husband had acquired this vicious disease, as he might have any of a dozen others, entirely independently of me, I soon stopped burdening myself with a feeling of guilt or self-pity for having chosen an alcoholic, with all the resultant problems and heartaches.

We have no supermen or superwomen in my group—we are a very commonplace gathering of ordinary persons, a fair cross-section of life today. But these ordinary people brought me my miracle. Living the Al-Anon program and following the Steps, we are cultivating God in ourselves and thus we are privileged to do His Work.

Picture of a Resentment

Is THERE EVEN one person alive who does not meet with an occasional upset? It may be of minor or major importance—a pinprick or a real blow but it is how we react to such upsets that we shape our lives: if the milk doesn't come in time for breakfast, do we snap at the children, are we short with our partners and generally dim the brightness of a new day? Or do we quickly realize that it is relatively unimportant and we can plan a substitute?

Generally speaking, it isn't what happens that counts, but what we do about it. If we allow things to affect us unduly, if we harp on what bothers us, we are fostering a resentment—we are allowing a pinprick to become a stab at our hearts.

People are not always careful to say exactly what they mean, so misunderstandings are bound to occur and wrong impressions are frequently given. Recently such a situation was created between two friends: one spoke quickly, the other was hurt and communication between them stopped. Immediately everything was magnified—each thought the other wrong; the first thought the second was being unreasonably difficult and the second that she was being taken advantage of. But each brooded over the other's attitude. That was a few weeks ago but by now everything the other does is examined in the light of a possible slight.

Instead of determining the original fault, as we do in Al-Anon, and accepting the responsibility for our share in it and making amends, each is carrying a grudge and fostering a resentment which is spoiling a friendship.

"Each day is a fresh beginning—each day is the world made new." If we teach ourselves to live actively with this approach to our daily intercourse with others, we'll really be practicing the Al-Anon program. We'll have no time nor wish to burden ourselves with yesterday's problems.

Are You in Your Second Childhood?

A FRIEND OF MINE once lamented that "it was practically impossible to keep a baby in the house. Before you realize it, they have become children."

Children also, grow up too fast, without knowing the wonderful things they leave behind them: their marvelous, built-in sense of justice for one thing, for who ever heard of children resenting punishment they knew they'd earned? Most lose their complete faith in their parents' power to guard them, for another, and their acceptance of all the world as a friend for a third.

We had these qualities once ourselves but somewhere along the dusty way we left them behind and took to resentments, hurt pride and a rat-race of worrying.

We have been told that we have only to ask for help and we shall receive it—that unless we become as little children we shall not enter the Kingdom of Heaven. What more do we need be told?

We know we have a Higher Power, ready to help us, just waiting to be called on. We cannot go back to our first childhood as we have shed too many skins since then, but there is a second childhood for all of us, which is a rebirth of faith and hope and trust. Let's hurry toward it.

Growing in Stature

"ALL TRULY WISE thoughts have been thought already thousands of times; but to make them really ours, we must think them over again honestly, till they take firm root in our personal experience."

I wish I had written that but Goethe did it first. There is nothing really new in our Program. It was taken whole-cloth from AA. AA got it in bits and pieces from the Sermon on the Mount, from the Oxford Movement and a dozen other sources. It was only new as AA and new as Al-Anon.

In our despair and heartbreak, it came to us as a life-and-sanity-saving, brand-new philosophy and we swallowed it whole, in great, stimulating gulps. What we understood, we put to work immediately and the wonder is that so much of it succeeded so quickly—most of us can easily think of dozens of newcomers who were completely changed by only a meeting or two.

But as we spent months and years following our Program, we absorbed more and more of it until we reached a deeper understanding; its teachings took "firm root in our personal experience."

This deeper understanding gave more and stronger support to us. Al-Anon's teachings enabled us to help others in the same state in which we once lived.

We didn't need anything new—we simply needed to make this truly great Program really ours by thinking and living it honestly.

Whose Story Do You Tell?

SOME TWO and a half thousand years ago, Joel exhorted his people "to rend your heart and not your garments." On a recent trip I was thinking of him as I listened to a couple of so-called "Al-Anon stories" at a meeting.

Two women spoke for a half hour each and it seems incredible that in that time neither mentioned what Al-Anon had done to help her.

Obviously the program had been successful with each, as both were fluent and poised—but each confined herself to her husband's drinking career and how nervous she had become.

To me it was unbelievable that they spent so much time rending their garments over what, happily for each, was over and done with, instead of searching their hearts for what had brought about a happy state.

Neither told anything new about a drinking career—after all, *is* there anything new to be said about one? Neither picked out one particular piece of the program and said, "This is how it worked for me and this is how I went about attacking my problem."

All of us have been in identical circumstances and it would help if we were told exactly how someone else benefited from applying the program.

Joel later promised that God "will restore to you the years that the locust hath eaten." Certainly no one will question that promise when he sees what miracles of tranquility the practice of this program brings to Al-Anon members.

But to those who still are entertaining the locusts, it is difficult to see how the miracle comes about. It would help tremendously if our members singled out the vital points of inspiration, the motivating ideas which aided them in their time of trial and made their talks about them.

Good Talks

As WE TOLD YOU last month, Al-Anon talks can be, and too often are, merely a repetition of past or present sorrows. It may be that such a talk helps the person giving it, though that is questionable, but certainly it is not the ideal speech.

Sketching the background is important and has its place, but it is merely the foundation of the whole talk.

The best talk, the one which helps most people to the highest degree, is the one which brings out just how the program works and how the speaker follows it.

Like Gaul, a good speech may be divided into three parts: "How sick I was. How well I am. What helped me to get well." Of those three parts the emphasis should be on what helped me get well: the Serenity Prayer, the First Step, the Inventory or whatever it was.

For some, a slogan did it and others found their help in the group spirit. But whatever started one of us to regain command of ourselves may well be the very thing to lead another into quiet waters.

The thing which impresses everyone new to Al-Anon is the utter honesty and simplicity of our members—it is never polished phrases which win adherents. We have no need of facile speakers; it may even be that too smooth a speech loses force, so that none of us need fear to talk when asked to do so.

All any of us needs is to spend enough time in analyzing how the program works; then words to tell of the miracle will come.

If one single phrase of a talk sheds light for another person that talk is a good one, though the speaker is halting in delivery. Ease in speaking comes with experience so we all improve with time.

Carrying the message to others, sharing our experiences, is the most important part of our 12th Step work and all we need to help us is some thoughtful time in preparing our talks.

Living the Program

NOTHING WAS EVER TRUER than that oldie, "You can't give what you haven't got." And it is particularly true of our Al-Anon program. If you do not live it yourself, you cannot show another person how to do so; tinkling cymbals and sounding brass are a full symphonic orchestra when compared with the chant of an Al-Anon member who gives only lip service to the program. Gaps and false notes inevitably come through.

If we say we are powerless over alcohol, and are turning our lives and will over to the care of God as we understand Him, and yet try to manage everything; if we ask God to remove our shortcomings and do nothing toward this end ourselves; if we hurt others and wholly ignore making amends; if we simply talk about the program during meetings and then forget it the rest of the time—nothing can cover up the emptiness of our words.

In the Army they say you can fool a General and all the other top brass but you can't fool the GIs. It is the same with us: we might fool someone who knows nothing about living with an alcoholic; we might appear saintly martyrs to outsiders but to those in great need of real help, unless we have grasped the truths we talk about, and applied them to our daily living, we are whistling in the wind.

An old Chinese proverb says, "If I hear it, I forget it; if I see it, I remember. If I do it, I know it." Only by living the program, day in and day out, can we really know it and only when we know the program can we give help to others.

When we have really "Let Go and Let God," have truly accepted "Thy Will, not mine," there is a quiet conviction which comes through even to those in the depths and they are lifted up. If we live this program, we can give it to others.

A Full Meal

IN JAPANESE prisoner-of-war camps, perhaps by necessity, rations finally shrank to a couple of ounces of rice a day. Our unhappy, starving prisoners pulled in their belts and dreamed of a full meal.

When liberation came, almost their first thought was, "Now we can have a full meal." So they might have, because the liberators brought plenty with them, but doctors said no—solid food in any quantity would make them sicker than they were and they must be physically conditioned to cope with a full meal.

Those people come to mind when I read or hear complaints about unanswered prayers. One way or another, many of us foul ourselves up with worldly cares until our spiritual tolerance is equivalent to a couple of ounces of rice.

Whether this sag comes because we are tried beyond our strength or because we lose perspective, is unimportant. Our prayers mostly are concerned with material things—better jobs, more money, a better place to live; the time for them is always NOW: we feel we deserve them and have a right to ask for them.

But think for a moment what would happen if all these prayers were granted simultaneously. Our Al-Anon program is one of spiritual growth and we know the Higher Power can restore us to sanity, but how ready would we be, were we suddenly deluged with material gifts?

It seems to me we cannot hope for overnight success—such growth in our blessings necessarily is slow; we must earn it. We must condition our spirits for it.

To me, the Higher Power is a great linguist, capable of translating every prayer into terms that are best for us: our cries for immediate, material help are answered, perhaps, with the gift of a little more patience with our lot in life; we are permitted to see that things of the spirit have more value than those of the body; we are given a true perspective.

I believe all the things we hope for will come to us when we are ready for them, when they will be for our real good—not now when they might enmesh us in more trouble.

If we accept the Higher Power as having greater wisdom than ours, and if we are willing to place His Will above our own, we then must wait until we are spiritually conditioned for our "full meal."

Faith and Hope

"Faith is the substance of things hoped for, the evidence of things not seen."

Although these words were written nearly two thousand years ago, men had lived by faith and hope long before the words ever were set down on parchment. Men are living by them now in these days of uneasy peace. And come what may, men will continue to live by them as long as they walk the earth.

Men must have faith and hope to endure life's hazards. Men have existed on minimum amounts of food and water, really too scant to sustain life, but as long as their spirits were strong, they hung on to a spark of life until relief came.

No one was mean enough to discourage the survivors of Bataan—no one could heartlessly disturb a child's faith that his mother can help him in all his troubles. Why, then, do we mortally wound ourselves by dimming our faith and hope for a better life?

We would not snatch hope from another's frantic grasp. We would not kill faith in any one eagerly seeking help. But we murder both in our own selves when we allow doubts of the alcoholic to muddy our thinking.

Al-Anon teaches us, and has proved many times over, that sobriety can be won by those who desire it enough; it has charted ways to help us through the dusty roads which lead eventually to our goal of happy, united homes; it offers a guide to serenity and self-mastery, which are priceless aids to daily living.

All this is ours if we throw ourselves wholeheartedly into our program. We can begin with only a spark of hope, a glimmer of faith—and through honest study and practice of Al-Anon thinking, we can foster that spark and that glimmer into a blaze of hope and faith which lights our lives and those about us.

What Really Counts

HAVE YOU EVER refrained from doing something you wanted to do or thought you should do, because you were "just one person and it wouldn't count"?

Even with hundreds of millions of persons on this earth, each one of us is separate and distinct from every other—one soon learns to differentiate even between identical twins.

And, with all the evidence that Creation was planned, not accidental happenstance, it seems to me that there's a reason for this wide diversity among individuals.

We believe a Power Greater Than Ourselves runs the universe, so it is easy to believe that, as each of us was made different, each of us was given different capabilities. I believe that each was given a job to do and the ability to do it, if we draw upon the Higher Power.

It may be that one line of one FORUM will deeply affect and help one person, and I shall have accomplished my job. It may be that one of your talks, at one meeting, will change the life of someone in the group, and your work will have been done.

I don't know what my job in life is, nor yours, but I do know we each have one. I know that only we can do our own job. Since we don't know when that opportunity comes, let's not pass up the chance to do it, by thinking, "I'm just one person who doesn't count." Rather let's think, "This is a job worth doing—I might be the only person in the world to do this specific thing."

Knowing Ourselves

IT FREQUENTLY has seemed to me that Villon was bragging when he wrote "I know all things, save myself." But, complex and individualistic as he was, for all I know he may have written it in a true spirit of deep humility: meant he knew all things save the most important one.

Certainly knowing ourselves is most important to us. Many of us first came to Al-Anon to find the non-existent secret of how to stop our mates' drinking. We thought there was a magic button we could learn to press and their lives and ours would be changed.

The lives of those of us in Al-Anon *were* changed but not by a magic button. We found we were powerless over alcohol and alcoholics, too, but learned to know ourselves and have kept on improving the acquaintance.

When we recognized the worry over a drinking partner as really an acute concern for our own security and well-being, when we saw that we ourselves were causing as much of our mental and physical turmoil as the alcoholic was doing, we were not proud, and soon learned we'd change ourselves only by studying and practicing the Twelve Steps.

Knowing ourselves shows that we didn't need to make scenes, nag or scold: that energy put into such nonsense was better used to strive for tranquility; serenity could be achieved if we worked at it.

We had come to think of ourselves as good managers and the only one in the family with sound judgment.

But Al-Anon showed us that, for all our good management, our lives still were unmanageable. It took the help of the Higher Power, and the humility to ask for that help, before our lives began to straighten out.

We discovered that frequently we had been Managing Mammas because we liked to be—now we see it often is more fun to sit beside the driver than to drive.

Not all that we learned about ourselves was bad. And, most important of all, we learned that we could learn. With every week of working the Al-Anon program we obtain deeper insight into ourselves and our families.

With new serenity and acceptance of others for what they are, we become more content and many of these new qualities brush off on our mates and help them to help themselves to lasting sobriety.

From Me to Me, with Love

GIVE YOURSELF the best Christmas present in the world—even if you are broke, you can afford it, though it is a priceless gift. In fact you can't afford not to give it to yourself.

This best of all possible gifts is a tranquil mind. You can't go out and buy it. You have to earn it for yourself with daily mental discipline and rigid self-control. Al-Anon has guideposts for you in the Serenity and in the St. Francis of Assisi prayers.

None of us would be in Al-Anon if our lives had run in smooth waters. We have real problems, I agree, but don't turn them into anxieties by churning them over and over. That way lies madness—many of us feared that's the way we were going, until Al-Anon. Fortunately we found that fellowship, and hope.

When we put honest thought and study into the program, we began to sort out the things we couldn't change; when we really worked the program we sought to accept those things; not to rebel against them. What we could change, we did.

But this is a continuing process. Basic problems have a way of changing from year to year so that we need to keep accepting—it's not an over-and-done-with job when we overcome one. We need to keep distinguishing those things we can change from those we can't. We can't always do this alone but we have a Higher Power waiting to lend a hand, just for the asking.

Whether or not you cause your own turmoil, only you can give yourself a tranquil mind and an accepting heart. Begin now, today, and by Christmas you'll be well on your way to that most priceless gift.

Our Program Has Everything

SOMETIMES OUR PROGRAM seems to me like the case of the preacher whose son was asked how his father could originate a different sermon every Sunday, and the boy lightly replied, "He doesn't—it's the same old one—he just hollers in different places."

Undoubtedly it is the same old program we follow: nothing has been changed in the Steps since they were adopted, and the slogans have been around a long time, too. But the good part about all of it is, that when a lift is needed, the program furnishes it.

When we are feeling frantically helpless, we are reminded that the Higher Power can help us; when we are feeling smug, the Inventory Step jumps up and flags our attention; when we are in a dizzy maze of futile wonderings, the Serenity Prayer calms us and reminds us to sort out the things we can change from those we can't and to ask for wisdom to know the difference. First Things First and Easy Does It are vital warnings when we tend to take in too much territory and are like children grabbing for everything in sight.

Whatever happens to us, some part of the program applies. All we need to do is quietly reflect a bit and the help we need will jump to our attention and "holler" in the right place.

An Invaluable Education

"THE BUSINESS of education is making people uncomfortable." At first glance such a statement sounds wholly ridiculous and unreasonable; but apply it to our program and it begins to make sense: before Al-Anon most of us quite smugly felt ourselves no less than perfect; any personal shortcoming quickly was dismissed with the self-pitying thought: "It's not my fault—it's because Joe drinks."

Too many sound people, in countless talks, have admitted feeling just that way, for us not to confess freely there were plenty of things wrong with us.

It took the education of Al-Anon to make us uncomfortable enough to sort out cause and effect and to realize the cause was not always someone else's drinking. It was a cause buried within us, perhaps from childhood, which had gradually emerged and grown until it could be recognized.

When people get uncomfortable enough about anything, the sensible person does something about it. So with Al-Anons and their self-pity, their nagging and their devious, behind-the-scenes efforts to manage partners.

Al-Anon teaches a hands-off policy—except on the body to which the hands are attached. Al-Anon teaches that self-pity is self-destructive beyond words, and any meeting furnishes proof enough that someone else is in worse case than we.

Al-Anon teaches that nagging is bad for the nagger but is hopeless for the nagee, so it's time worse than wasted.

If Al-Anon education makes us thoroughly uncomfortable, uncomfortable enough so that we begin to study the program, then it truly is an invaluable education.

Failure Has Its Place

THE IDEA THAT HE, or she, is less than perfect, seldom dawns on the neophyte. But even within the span of a few weeks, enough of the Al-Anon program penetrates one's thinking so thoroughly that we get caught with our imperfections showing.

Essentially perfection is what we are striving for. We

must try to put ourselves in perfect accord with our God and our fellow man.

Progress toward that goal is measured by the amount of thought and action we put into the program. If we confine Al-Anon thinking and practice to meeting nights, progress can be made—because the program is one of growth—but it will be slow.

However, if we channel our efforts toward absorbing as much of the program as we are able to do, day by day, we'll get there faster.

No one, even after years of practice, ever lives our philosophy completely, all of the time. Human error thrusts itself in, and we sometimes become irritated or angry. If we were living the program in its entirety, we'd have enough vision to overcome these interruptions to our serenity.

But however far we fall short of our goal, if we have grasped even a minor part of the program we still have made progress. Each small success in practicing it makes the next one easier.

The thing we need to be conscious of is that we all fail sometimes. It's not how badly we fail nor how wantonly, that counts. To recognize that through failing we learn where we should be alert for danger is the important thing. If we accept these failures as challenges to further growth, then they will serve as steps to success.

Comparison Shopping

HAVE YOU EVER made a comparison-inventory of your own progress and accomplishments, through Al-Anon, and your partner's progress and accomplishments, through AA?

Each of us in Al-Anon realizes that we are not the only one singled out to bear almost intolerable burdens. We realize, too, that the alcoholic also has his own frightful burden and his own private war.

We start even, more or less, from there. But beyond that, the two problems are completely different—poles apart, in fact.

The alcoholic is suffering from one of the world's most insidious diseases and is fighting a twenty-four hour daily battle against a compulsion almost beyond his strength.

We are free of the physical aspects of the disease but none the less are fighting twenty-four hours daily against real, tough, heartbreaking situations.

The big difference is that we have the advantage of being able to fight with a more or less normal outlook: at least it is not complicated by a driving urge to do something against our will.

Sure, sober alcoholics still are difficult to live with. But ask yourself which of us, even without the alcoholic's specific ailment and handicaps, is a constant dream of delight?

So, the next time your mate irritates you thoroughly, pause, consider, do a little comparison-shopping. Ask yourself if you are making as much, or more progress, as he or she is, in the daily battle to win victory, to earn a big share of the new way of life.

Strength

"IN QUIETNESS and in confidence shall be thy strength." What better goal could we have than quiet, confident strength? Think about the older members of your group, who have really studied our Al-Anon program and made it part of their daily lives, and you will have proof that this goal can be attained.

You weren't around when they first came to meetings, so you can't tell whether they were the kind who talked incessantly, monopolizing meetings, or the walled-in kind who said nothing. Each variety presents its own difficulties but perhaps it's a little easier to help someone when you know what's bothering him.

But whether his complaints flowed incessantly like a mountain torrent or, like me, were silently shrieked inside a tightly-shut clamshell, each of us came to Al-Anon for help.

We were an unattractive mess of self-pity, out of touch and out of kilter with ordinary life. We were the only one whose laundryman didn't come; the only one whose child caught cold; the only one married to a sot—everything had equal power to upset us.

It was only when we could stand ourselves no longer that we really exposed ourselves to Al-Anon. We, too, "hit bottom" and the only way out was up.

We relaxed a little, our minds opened a fraction to what we were told and gradually a healthy, hopeful outlook was regained. We stopped complaining, either verbally or silently. Some part of the program, the First Step, Serenity Prayer or a slogan made sense and we began with that and went on to other parts.

Before too long, maybe months and maybe a year or so, we found ourselves possessed of an inner quietness and confidence which we could depend on to be strong enough to see us through anything. If you have not yet reached this goal for yourself, be very sure that it nevertheless is there to be reached: quiet confidence in yourself, your mate, in life and in the Higher Power will be your strength and it will carry you through.

Time to Think

RECENTLY I HAD a most inconvenient, painful and frightening experience: all I did was take a single step on bad curbing and I ended up with my best foot forward in a fifteen-pound cast.

The next eleven days I spent in the hospital, thinking it over. That accident couldn't have happened at a worse time: it came square in the middle of a week's meetings which had been planned for nearly a year.

Ten minutes before it happened, I'd have said that nothing on earth could have prevented my attendance but I missed all of it and lived through it.

No one who knows me would ever confuse me with a Pollyanna, but just eleven days, with plenty of time to think, gave me some new outlooks on life.

For one thing, I developed flu but since bedrest is indicated for that, and I was in bed anyhow, I got over it much more quickly and completely than I'd have done at home. I was right there, handy, when it was time for penicillin shots. There were nurse's aides to see that I drank plenty of juices and took my pills. So I recovered in record time. One bonus for the accident.

The second was the time to think, of which I spoke. When I got over my initial self-pity, I had time to think how fortunate I was that, landing as I did, I hadn't broken both wrists as well as my foot and have been completely helpless. I had time to thank God that no car had been coming along or I'd have been run over. I had time to thank Him I'd got off so easily.

And I went on to think that such things may not necessarily be accidental—perhaps I needed such a thing to jolt my thinking . . . as perhaps I'd also needed the jolts of living with an alcoholic to throw me out of an accustomed rut into the searchings and disciplines of Al-Anon.

I decided that things happen for the best if we ourselves do not waste our opportunities, if we search for the good in every experience and put it to use.

Had I lived a tranquil, normal life, I'd probably be unbearably smug; had I not found Al-Anon, I'd likely have become a shrew and at best would have matured only partially.

It came to me that, just as my accident was not wholly waste, neither was the unhappiness I had endured, if I myself did not allow it to be.

There's Always a Last One

IT IS DIFFICULT to imagine a shock greater than one receives if a partner has had some success on the AA program and then suffers a slip. To the normal person, free of the awful compulsion to drink, the AA program is so logical and foolproof that ignoring it seems wantonly extravagant and wilful. It is impossible to understand why anyone would trifle with such a plan.

Fortunately, he doesn't have to understand. But he does have to accept, and our Al-Anon program and emphasis on the Steps help in this acceptance. And even while the slip is taking place, the Al-Anon member is in much better case than ever before: he has a fellow-member to whom to turn for help and in whom to confide if he is driven to confiding.

There are meetings to attend, where one can obtain help and guidance. There are the Al-Anon books to read and the many helpful booklets.

And since AA helps nearly nine out of every ten members, there is the great percentage that one's partner will be one of the fortunates. These fortunates all stop drinking some time, and one can always hope that this slip will be the last one.

What We're Here For

IT SEEMS CERTAIN to me that we were put into this world to grow in two directions: first physically and second, but most important, spiritually. Otherwise our Creator would have planned differently and, if my mythology is sound, we'd perhaps spring, like Minerva, from the forehead of Jove. As it is we grow from helpless, speechless infants; it takes months and years to learn to walk easily from here to there or to make ourselves quickly understood. It's a long process to adulthood.

We are not creatures of accident. We were created by that Higher Power, whom I call God, and He surely put us here to grow. God doesn't *find* good in us accidentally—rather He puts good in us and gives us the privilege of fostering and increasing it. Whenever we let life get us down—so that we do mean or careless things to others—we defeat our primary purpose in life; we shrink rather than grow.

When we live Al-Anon sincerely and fully, practice the Twelve Steps as perfectly as we are able, we grow up spiritually, too, and fulfill the purpose for which we are here.

A Sourdough's Self Discipline

YEARS AGO, before Al-Anon or even AA, a friend of mine set his private plane down in the back-country of Alaska. There he met up with an old "sourdough" who taught him a lesson he never forgot—one which has stayed with me for many, many years—and incidentally is one of the backbone maxims of our fellowship.

During Bob's two-day visit with the old bachelor in his primitive cabin hundreds of miles from nowhere, he learned that his host received his mail—regularly, all in one huge batch—on one day, each year! The mail consisted mostly of his hometown daily newspapers.

Bob said, "When all those papers arrive, I bet you have a field day, poring through them to catch up on what's been happening."

"Oh no," the old fellow replied, "Quite the contrary. That way it would be all over in a few days. No, sir! I just make myself take it easy . . . I live my life one day at a time. First, I sort them according to date, with the oldest papers first. Then each morning at breakfast, for the whole year, I have a fresh newspaper and they last until the next delivery."

He never slipped—even when there was a murder or an investigation of something hot. He never peeked ahead at the next day's edition to see what was going to "happen." It was all news to him and he made it last.

Somehow he's never really been out of my mind in the years since Bob told me about him. I have always admired his self-discipline in waiting and making his papers last.

I know we need the same sort of self-discipline as that old sourdough in his back-country cabin. I believe we need to live each day as it comes, determined that just for that day we won't let our Al-Anon principles slip from mind but make sure to practice them perfectly. If we do this every day, one day at a time, we will make the program last the year 'round for us too!

All Human Beings Make Mistakes

A LITTLE BOY answered the doorbell one day, invited the visitor into the house, hunted up his mother and said there was someone in the living room. When asked who it was, he replied, "I don't know, but I believe it is a human being."

If we were all more ready to accept ourselves and each other as human beings, there'd be more happiness and less tension in our lives. Certainly we should aim at perfection—should not take failures with complacence. We should evaluate them to discover the cause, but not be crushed by them.

Have you ever stopped to think that a lot of trouble can be caused for yourself, or for others, by expecting too much? Either way leads to heartaches and headaches.

If you rely on a notoriously careless friend to do an exacting job, you'll feel let down if nothing much is accomplished. If you plan to do a dozen things in one day but only finish ten, you are left with a sense of failure.

But perhaps you should have chosen a different person for the exacting task and should have scheduled fewer things for yourself.

Groups, too, get into difficulties because some members expect perfection in all the others: they say, "After all, we are striving for spiritual growth and if those members 'have got the program,' why do they act that way?"

I believe it's quite possible that those people do "have the program" but just slipped momentarily and it shouldn't be held against them.

If we had the program better ourselves we mightn't be annoyed at others. They are human beings.

Browning said, "A man's reach should exceed his grasp, or what's a heaven for?" So, if we constantly, and quite properly, reach for perfection, we shouldn't castigate ourselves and others for constantly falling short.

If we remember that only God makes no mistakes, we can accept ourselves, and our fellowmen, as human beings, with much more happiness and contentment all around.

Counting Our Blessings

WHY ARE WE so often afraid of seeming to be sentimental or complacent if we congratulate ourselves for what we have gained from our Al-Anon philosophy? Are we afraid of being thought Pollyannas, or "corny?" Or do we think we have no reason for congratulations?

Many Al-Anon members are married to still-active alcoholics; many have spent a dozen or more years with a drinking problem which has just lately been resolved.

Scars are deep but the wounds are not mortal hurts. Perhaps if they were examined in a true light, they would prove to mark opportunities for spiritual growth, and so are like a soldier's battle ribbons. Growth seldom is accomplished without pain.

Once in a while, it seems to me, we'd do well to meditate for a moment and simply count our blessings—forget the failings—and dwell on what we have that is good.

No matter how bad the drinking problem is, we are at least alive to cope with it. And just being alive is our first blessing.

A Blast of Fresh Air

A SEXTON had difficulty heating the church and when the minister complimented him on the comfortable warmth he finally achieved, the sexton said, "I shoveled and shoveled and couldn't get the heat to 50. Then I opened all the doors and windows and it got frigid. But when I had thoroughly aired the church and shut it up again, the temperature went right up to 70."

If you've been stewing around in an uncomfortable bog of "bills, bills, bills" or "kids, kids, kids" or even "drunks, drunks, drunks," why not try the sexton's trick? Stop everything and let a blast of fresh air into your mind. You aren't getting anywhere, anyhow, just by worrying.

Blank your mind of whatever it is that is nagging at you. Then take a new, quiet look at it, ask the Higher Power for help and you'll find your answer.

If We Choose

STEPHEN VINCENT BENET once wrote, "Our earth is but a small star in the great universe. Yet of it we can make, if we choose, a planet unvexed by war, untroubled by hunger or fear, undivided by senseless distinctions . . ." I believe he was dead right but that it will take some doing to make such a world.

I believe each one of us is but an infinitesimal part of the billions who inhabit our "small star in the great universe," but we are an important part and, if we choose, we can make our lives count toward ending war, hunger, fear and the divisions of senseless distinctions among us.

I believe, if we choose, we can conquer fear and to me, that is the place to begin. I believe this also takes some doing. It was fear which made us the wrecks we were when we came to Al-Anon—fear of the past, present and future, of public and private opinion, of ourselves and of our mates and of the world at large.

By following the program as it gradually unfolds, by practicing the Steps more honestly and whole-heartedly, we gradually overcome these fears. Like all human beings, we have failures because we sometimes falter in these observances and fear returns.

We do know, however, that fear can be vanquished by constant effort. We know that life without fear is a heavenly blessing and the whole world is a different place when we have peace of mind. We can have these things, if we choose.

Learning from Experience

"EXPERIENCE IS THE best teacher" has been around too long not to have a lot of truth in it. It would have been forgotten long since if it didn't make sense.

"Experience is the best teacher," certainly—but whose experience, is the question. Having the same old ones, for twenty years, maybe—"Joe's drunk again"—obviously didn't teach many of us how to cope with it, how to live with it, for a long time.

What we need, when we come to Al-Anon, is to gain experience in a big, big way—and fast.

We can learn more ways to handle our situation from a dozen group meetings, than we previously did in a decade. Going it alone is a long hard road because it involves making the same old mistakes.

What we need is to learn how experienced Al-Anoners have handled situations similar to ours, how they have handled themselves successfully.

Definitely, we can learn by experience. But that experience need not be our own.

A "Do It Yourself" Method for Al-Anon

"MANY PEOPLE are unhappy in marriage because they expected to get too much with too little effort," counseled David R. Mace, in discussing rocky marriages.

Just change "marriage" to "Al-Anon," and this could have been written about some members and some groups.

We have all seen a number of people attend a few meetings; sit back passively and neither participate in discussions nor try to follow the program.

Then they stay away because they were disappointed. They expected to get too much, for too little effort. In fact, they had expected to find the magic key to a mate's sobriety, in answer to the simple question, "How do you make some one stop drinking?"

We know there's no answer to that question. But we do know that through Al-Anon, we can find peace for ourselves—even though the drinking continues, and furthermore, that frequently our own peace impinges upon the alcoholic and he seeks peace for himself, through AA.

Groups, too, sometimes expect too much for too little effort. Keeping a group active and healthy takes serious work by each and every member; they have to contribute ideas, leadership and time.

No group can grow and broaden its influence if everything is left to one or two, or even five or six, members. Actually, it takes considerable time for a group to develop to its fullest usefulness. But even if one remains small, for months or indeed for years, who is to say that that group is not aiding its members?

Many groups always will be small for one reason or another, but nevertheless they still can exert great influence.

Let's really apply a "Do It Yourself" Al-Anon method for ourselves and also for our groups, so that we'll never expect too much, for too little effort.

First Things First

ONE OF THE very first things that struck us, in Al-Anon, with terrific force, was that we were not all alone in the turmoiled world of alcoholism. We had thought that we alone had been singled out to cope with a bewildering problem.

We even thought that wilfulness, lack of self-control, or just plain cussedness, was responsible for excessive drinking and we were ashamed and confused. In our sick despair, most of us had crawled into a hole and tried to pull as much of it in after us as was possible. But at Al-Anon we found scores of others, each with the selfsame problem. That gave us our first, immediate lift.

Then came the revelation that alcoholism definitely is a disease! We learned further that while this disease positively cannot be cured, still it can be arrested and that gave us hope.

For some of us that hope was dampened from time to time, when a partner, having sought and found AA help, returned to uncontrolled drinking. Still others had hope dimmed when a partner refused to recognize that there was a problem and continued to drink excessively.

But the knowledge that a disease was responsible helped us to see the whole problem in a different perspective.

One thing we can never learn in Al-Anon is to understand the tremendous compulsion to continue drinking that an alcholic has, once one drop of alcohol is imbibed. Only another alcoholic can understand that.

Also we can never learn, at Al-Anon or anywhere else for that matter, how to stop an alcoholic's drinking. That definitely is his problem and only he can solve it.

With the help of others similarly situated, and with the hope we get from knowing that approximately 300,000 problem drinkers have found a new life in AA, we learn to stop our frantic efforts to force sobriety upon our mates.

We learn to turn our energies upon ourselves, and to accept what we cannot change in others. First Things First means, for us, that our first responsibility is to ourselves and it is upon ourselves that each of us works in Al-Anon.

Quality of Prayer

MANY TIMES at our own, as well as at AA meetings, I have heard people talk of "gimme prayers" as if they were worthless. Speaking only for myself, I believe they could not be more wrong because I cannot think God considers any prayer worthless.

Just as most children creep before they walk, and walk

before they run, so we progress spiritually from "gimme" prayers to selfless ones where we ask only to know God's Will and to follow it. No one says the child is wasting his time creeping—he's learning, just as we have to learn to pray.

Further, I cannot see that it is wrong to ask for material help, when the Lord's Prayer itself contains our plea for daily bread. I believe we get beyond the point of asking for purely material things just as some of our members are able to thank God for their having married an alcoholic and thus learning about our program. In all honesty, I'd have been glad to be spared that: some day I may attain this peak but I do thank Him for what acceptance I have managed to develop.

Prayer, to me, is a learning process. If we put our hearts and minds into praying properly, I am sure we progress in the spiritual quality of prayer. Some prayers are more deeply meaningful than others, and thus more valuable, but I am convinced that any prayer at all is better than none.

Make Straight the Way

A LONG TIME AGO a voice in the wilderness cried, "Prepare ye the way of the Lord, make His paths straight. Every valley shall be filled, and every mountain and hill shall be brought low; and the crooked shall be made straight and the rough ways shall be made smooth."

We may have heard these words frequently, without realizing that in ancient times, much of this actually was done when a king visited. All the people leveled paths through hills and mountains, filled valleys, smoothed roads.

This straightening the way was done a hundred years ago when American railroads pushed rights-of-way across the country. And even today we repeat the process with gigantic roadbuilding projects.

We are not engineers and only use the roads—so what has this to do with Al-Anon? Well, we all have our personal mountains and valleys within us and rough roads to be made smooth. We came into Al-Anon for many reasons but remained for the serenity we found.

We have accumulated mountains of resentments. Some are well overgrown with the green of envy of others more fortunately placed. We have valleys of despair into which we sometimes fall. No road is smooth when strewn with self-pity and ill will.

Al-Anon is the road to "the Higher Power which we call God." Let us then make straight the way: no bulldozer can level the mountain of resentment but straight thinking can push it away.

Fill the Valley of Despair with hope, and rise above immediate limitations. Say the Serenity Prayer and change rebellion to acceptance.

Remember that "This, too, shall pass," and forget to dwell on how horrible this life is.

Few things smooth roads, or brighten lives as much as helping others: if we forget self and remember to do things for others, we'll soon be on our own smooth road.

So, let's make straight the way. All we need is the will to do it—for Al-Anon has given us the blueprint.

Al-Anon Has Answers

WHAT DO YOU DO when you're sizzling angry? If someone has offended you, do you blast back at that person? Do you freeze up into an outraged icicle? Or do you concentrate on "paying him back?"

Over the years I've either tried or seen all these methods used and never much admired any. I'd always got away as fast as possible when angered and then pitched into a job I usually put off because I hate it, like cleaning out the refrigerator or degreasing the oven . . . anything I could put my back into. For me, this worked fairly well but now I've progressed.

Al-Anon has mental aids to calmness and control: the Serenity Prayer comes first. Even though I begin saying it with lip service only, I keep repeating it like "a rose is a rose is a rose." Somewhere along the line, one of the ideas catches up, either the idea of God and then my "mad" seems petty, or I wonder if what happened is a thing I can or can't change and I go on to the courage part.

The slogans are a handy tool too: Easy Does It is always applicable. I can't tell myself to take it easy if I'm yelling. First Things First is good too. I stop to think what really caused the fracas; I may have contributed to it and if I recognize I helped start the fire, I can't be eager to add more fuel.

Somewhere in Al-Anon's teachings there's an answer. It may not be an easy one. But any answer is better than keeping on at a full rolling boil.

Squares and Grannys—In and Out of Al-Anon

DO YOU EVER tie a square knot, but pull and find it's a granny? That's what I usually do; only on the third or fourth try, do I get my square knot. If I didn't know better, I'd swear I do exactly the same thing each time— they just turn out differently.

Whenever my square knot turns out a granny, precisely

the same thought pops into my mind: this is why people have trouble with the program; this is why they question if Al-Anon always works.

They think they're giving it the same attention as always, following suggestions as carefully as usual and giving the program first place in their thoughts. But I don't believe they are.

When Al-Anons get discouraged this way, I believe they've allowed other things to creep in to distract them, so that they've taken a wrong turn, just as I've done with my string.

Maybe they've left Al-Anon at the door of the meeting room and are not using it in their daily lives.

When Al-Anon thinking dominates our daily lives, when God is left to run His world, which He created, in the way He wants it run, then we have no need to question the results. Everything falls into its proper place; there are no wrong turnings and our square knots are always square.

Who Can "Carry the Message?"

TO CARRY the message of Al-Anon to others is one of the greatest privileges and most rewarding experiences of our entire program. But remember, "You can't give what you haven't got." In order to communicate the message successfully, there are three basics:

First, that you know and accept and can prove that our message is authentic, intelligent and effective. Since all Al-Anon teaching emphasizes that we are in this program to grow spiritually ourselves, your message will be distorted if you are still seeking only a way to sobriety for your mate. That is not authentic Al-Anon, although it's what brought most members into the fellowship originally.

The effectiveness of Al-Anon's program is demonstrated in any meeting of a serious group which is really working at it: just contrast the serenity of even a three-months member with the confused turmoil of a newcomer.

As for the intelligence of the program, no stupidity or blind spots could persist in it with so many people giving it the real workout they do; the strength and growth of our movement proves its sense.

Second basic is that you study and actually live the program in every way. You may know that alcoholism is a disease, but if you continue to act resentfully and to permit self-pity in yourself, your message of hope to another will be meaningless.

Third basic is that you carry the message to others in language they understand. Successful communication is a two-way deal; unless one gives and another receives, the message is lost. If your belief in Al-Anon is strong and clear, you don't need eloquence to put it in deathless prose—the meaning will get across.

Al-Anon philosophy is simple. It is a program for spiritual growth; we work it for the benefit we obtain from it, and joyfully accept any side-benefits it brings. Of ourselves, we are frequently helpless but we have a Higher Power upon whom we can always rely.

So, equipped with this sure knowledge and the inspiration of the Higher Power, YOU can carry the message.

Who's a Failure?

IF YOU'VE NEVER been discouraged, never felt that really living the Al-Anon program is beyond you, then these ideas are not for you. They are for those persons who, tried beyond their strength, slip a bit in control and revert to pre–Al-Anon behavior.

A very large number of our members are married to active alcoholics; they have come to Al-Anon, have found help in it and a measure of serenity. For the most part, they are able to manage themselves well, keep fairly quiet when the alcholic activity is most active. But occasionally something gives—and they let go.

Does this mean they "haven't got the program?" It may, but I don't believe it has to mean that. I believe it means they are human beings. I'm always sorry when I hear or read of an Al-Anoner becoming discouraged because he's blown his top under considerable provocation.

I think the thing to do under these circumstances is to get one's self in hand as quickly as possible, go back to Al-Anon and AA first principles, and stop feeling we are worthless and our Al-Anon work has been in vain.

To me, the Higher Power means God, and I believe He made the world and the men in it. I believe He also made angels. But I'm sure He made the two different: when He created angels, He made them pure spirits, but to man He gave human nature and free will. Since I'm certain He knew what He was doing, I'm also certain He does not expect the same things of each.

Angels were made perfect at the beginning but to man is given the chance to approach perfection. If man takes two steps forward and slips half a step back, I do not believe God brands him a failure; I believe He gives him courage to try again, to do a little better than before.

If I'm even only half right (and, as always, these chats here are purely my personal opinions) I think it a great pity to allow discouragement to overwhelm one and to accept the burden of defeat.

It makes sense to me that if God had wanted man to be

perfect with no effort of his own, He'd have created him that way.

As long as we keep trying for perfection, even though we miss it occasionally, or even frequently, if the effort is honest and sincere, I don't think God considers us failures.

Failure is in giving up, in not trying—the rest, I believe, is just the human nature God gave us which is our opportunity for spiritual growth.

The Glory of Al-Anon

THERE ARE MANY wonderful things about Al-Anon but to me, one of the most remarkable, and yet the most characteristic, is the feeling that "You are a stranger here but once."

To most of us, twenty minutes after we have walked into an Al-Anon meeting, be it in Orleans, Massachusetts, or Missoula, Montana, there is a sense of being completely at home and of being at ease with people exactly like ourselves.

We may not immediately grasp why these crazy people laugh at tragedy, such as our pitiful tale of a mate who hides bottles, breaks promises and spends rent money on a binge. But, somehow, we sense there is understanding in that laughter and it is not long before we can eke out a smile ourselves.

We may not find ourselves in complete accord with every person in the group, but that is not necessary. If there is just a single person there to whom we spark, that is sufficient—that person can shed light in our dark places and lift us over the humps.

Should you find yourself completely out of sympathy

with an entire group, and if you live where there are others, why not try another and perhaps find you like it better?

But if there is no other group available, either start a new one or try digging in your heels and find something you like about the one you are in. Go to at least six meetings before you decide the group is not for you.

The glory of Al-Anon is that there's something in it for everyone; while you are learning about the program, the others are learning, too, and perhaps you'll find you misjudged some of them at first.

Steps to Heaven

I AM ABOUT as musical as a cow but music has always interested me. Odd bits and pieces of it stick in my mind and I love stories about it.

Take Debussy and his "Gradus au Parnassum," from the Children's Corner: I wouldn't have known, myself, that the whole thing is made up of fingering exercises and scales, to improve technique. He just put them together in such a way that a real, musical composition resulted whereby children could be trapped into the best kind of practice, all the time thinking they were "playing a piece."

Maybe the smart ones who knew Latin figured out that the title "Steps to Heaven" boiled down to "practice makes perfect" but they improved, too, as they played.

And that's where I am grateful to Debussy and his sly imagery. For years I have thought of our 12 Steps as Steps to Heaven. We must practice them diligently unless we are to revert to our previous discord.

In this constant practice we strengthen our technique for harmonious, sane living. Given enough time and effort on working the Steps and a healthy, confident self-command will result just as surely as running scales will help a pianist.

We are not children. We do not have to be trapped into practicing this program. Just remembering the hell we made for ourselves of life before it, is enough to keep it in the forefront of our minds. But thinking of it as our Steps to Heaven is a very happy thought to me.

No Little Plans

"MAKE NO little plans. They have no magic to stir men's blood and, probably, of themselves, will not be realized. Aim high in hope and work, remembering that a noble diagram once recorded will never die, but long after we are gone, will be a living thing."

Daniel Hudson Burnham was an architect so he did not have me in mind when he wrote that but it's been one of my three "words to live by."

"The way to spiritual growth is to do two impossible things a day" and "A man's reach should exceed his grasp or what's a Heaven for?" are the other two. All three have the same idea and the same spur: a man needs to stretch himself, to be bigger than he naturally is; he may not be comfortable in the stretching but if he settles just for comfort, he may as well have remained an infant who yells when he's damp or hungry.

There is a certain potential in each person but it is developed by conscious effort, by aiming at being bigger and better than he normally is, not by preoccupying one's self with just getting by.

That's where Al-Anon's program is such a tremendous stimulation. No one could even half-live it without being a better person and, for those who really practice it in all their daily affairs, there is a satisfaction beyond physical comfort, a deep spiritual appreciation of true values and a mental ease which is Heaven itself after the turmoil in which we once permitted ourselves to live.

Practicing the 12 Steps perfectly is no little goal. It is a splendid and tremendous one at which to aim. And if Heaven is beyond our immediate grasp, in practicing the Steps as well as we are able, we catch glimpses of it which give new impetus to our search for serenity.

Arise and Walk

"SON, be of good cheer. Thy sins are forgiven thee . . . Arise and walk." These lines from Matthew (9, 1:8) come to us from nearly two thousand years ago but still they indicate priorities in Al-Anon. When the man "sick of the palsy" was brought before Christ, He "saw his faith and was moved to compassion." But which did He cure first, body or spirit?

And just as the paralytic's spiritual house was put in order before he was restored to physical health, so do we have to do in Al-Anon. If we simply go through the physical motions of the program by putting a curb unwillingly on our tongues, grudgingly feed the alcoholic, attend meetings only for the chance to complain or so that we may say, "I did *everything* I could," we are handicapping ourselves.

If an unfortunate situation endures very long, most of us show physical deterioration: insomnia, extreme nervous exhaustion, elevated blood pressure. Doctors help some but usually not enough. It is when some gleam penetrates our spiritual darkness, when we surmount our self-pity and resentment, when we "clean house," mentally and spiritually that we really begin to benefit from Al-Anon.

Along with shedding our spiritual trash, we lighten ourselves of an intolerable burden. Peace, serenity and acceptance follow so that we are released from crippling fears and can "arise and walk" with confidence and hope.

Gifts of Al-Anon

HOLIDAY TIME is a season of giving and all of us try to give gifts which will be useful, exciting, pleasing, welcome: gifts which will express our love.

That takes a lot of thought. We just can't walk into the first store we come to and, beginning with Anne at the top of our list, go right down to Warren, picking the first thing we see for each one.

"The gift without the giver is bare," and in this case our thought and our concern for exactly the right gift is a large part of the giver.

Fortunately Al-Anon's season extends through the whole year, through the whole world. And exactly the same qualities apply to Al-Anon's gifts. If we try to give another person hope and serenity, merely by mouthing its principles and slogans, our gift indeed is bare.

We have to give of ourselves: our experience, our methods and our conclusions. We have to give enough thought to what that other person has gone through, his feelings at the moment, and what will best help him glimpse his own capabilities, to enable us to choose exactly the right things to say to him.

We don't have to have golden words at our command. We don't have to be brilliant. We don't have to be wealthy in worldly goods.

We just have to care enough about Al-Anon and that "other" person, truly to give of ourselves. We have received Al-Anon's gifts in abundance. Let us bestow them with love, for it is our precious opportunity to help make the world a lot better for having had these gifts ourselves. "God bless us every one," and happy holidays to all.

From Me, to You, with Love

Father, help me to face issues, not to avoid them for fear of what others may say. Let me be willing to take risks, let me not be afraid of blunders. Give me courage to speak, even when I know I shall do it badly, and let me always believe in laughter as the solvent for self-pity. I pray also for grace to suffer fools gladly, especially that one which is myself. From "Prayers for a Busy Day."

What better way is there to begin a new year than with a prayer such as the one above? It is my New Year's gift to you. I hope you find in it all the things we in Al-Anon so frequently need, so badly.

It might almost seem that this prayer had been written for Al-Anon, for people like you and me who have so often shunted disagreeable issues around in our minds, afraid to face them and to settle them; afraid of risks, of mistakes, afraid of everything, in fact.

And even after we have been in Al-Anon for some time, many of us are still afraid to speak, exactly as the prayer says, because "I know I shall do it badly."

What if we make no hit at first? Polished oratory is not

expected at Al-Anon. If we don't make every intended point, in our first attempt, but have courage to try again, then we'll do better for having pulled ourselves together, put more thought on it, and got up and given it.

Laughter we find in Al-Anon, just as soon as we relax a bit and regain our perspective. And tolerance for suffering fools gladly is everywhere about us; we just have to learn to save a little for ourselves.

With or without this prayer, may you find serenity and happiness in the new year.

Patience Is a Virtue—and a Goal

EPITAPHS SEEM to have gone out of style. Folks settle now for just names and dates. But some of the old ones are well worth pondering. Take for instance, "Here lies a patient man." At first thought that doesn't seem like very much to say of a whole lifetime of living.

But think for a moment. Just what goes into patience? Surely it's not just gritting one's teeth and bearing discomfort, not just putting up with dullness, not just lulling one's self into a soothing stupor.

Patience is made up of much more: faith, hope, love, courage.

Without faith and hope, few of us could bear to contemplate tomorrow. This was just as true when Columbus sought a new route to the Indies as it is today, when we seek freedom from the H-bomb threat.

Without love, man wouldn't be bothered with anything but himself. Why should he be, if nothing means anything to him?

And certainly courage is a big part of patience: courage

to go on when life is difficult; courage to accept disappointment; courage just to go on being one's self, even in a humdrum way.

Patience is far from the negative virtue it seems at first. To have patience really is an all-time job, an all-day job, an every day goal to aim at. When we consider God's patience with us and our nonsense, we should be filled with determination to be more patient with Him and with our "neighbors"—and with ourselves!

Look Around You

EACH OF US needs something bigger than ourself to fall back upon, to carry us through each day. That's a cliché, but just pause and realize how true it is. Clichés ARE clichés because they represent universal experience.

It's not accidental that people speak of being down in the dumps or up on a cloud—most of us are exhilarated by heights and depressed by depths.

The fortunate ones among us find the something bigger within themselves: a spiritual outlook, a philosophy of life which carries them through. The others could, if they looked searchingly enough, find inspiration all about them.

During World War II we were stationed on an Air Base in Nebraska. The vast, level prairies drove some of our friends nearly out of their minds. They deplored the dreariness, the monotony.

But I loved the prairies. There was something exciting about being able to see all the way to the horizon, across land as flat as the runways. It was thrilling to look up to a sky as big as the earth, with not even a corner cut off by hills, nor hemmed in by buildings. The endless vista stirred my imagination and lifted my spirits.

Even in man-made New York there are things that lift the spirit, catch at the throat. Turn a corner and there's a church steeple with a single star hanging beside it; there's the sweep of a wide avenue in the rain with the glistening reflection of a thousand street lamps.

No matter where you are, you don't have to search for the something bigger within yourself, especially when you are unhappy. Look around you. Find something to make you stretch yourself, reach out of yourself. The lift it gives, and the peace it leaves, will carry you through the day.

We Need Your Thought, Help and Prayers

THIS APRIL FORUM begins with our soon-to-be-held World Service Conference, and it is ending with it, which does not really mean that we're going in circles at Headquarters. It simply indicates just how important is this phase of our development.

There was a time when Al-Anon was small enough and close enough for us to keep in touch with each other by means of what we called the "Clearing House." We tried to make that group as representative as possible, as interested in Al-Anon and as dedicated to its growth and perpetuation as we could. But groups then numbered less than a hundred and our world-impact was a lone group in England. Today we have not too many less than two thousand groups, all over the map, all with problems, all with interest in Al-Anon, all of them made up of individuals with a common, unhappy experience.

Like AA, in which we have our roots, one of our most

cherished beliefs is that the individual and the groups have the right to take what is wanted from the program. Every group is autonomous; every member's opinion is his own. We believe the less organization we have, the better it is.

These things we believe and cherish dearly. But we also are concerned that Al-Anon will endure. We see that, left to themselves, some groups may so change our program to suit themselves and to meet present (and perhaps transient) needs, that all Al-Anon may be affected: diluted, altered and hamstrung.

It is because we feel so heartily that Al-Anon must remain universal, cohesive and strong, that we are broadening the influence of those who guide it. The "group conscience" we so greatly rely upon must be as representative as possible, as broad as we can make it.

So, as we begin our Second World Service Conference, we need your help, your thoughts and your prayers for its success. We count on you, all over the world, to armor us as we meet.

Death and Taxes

THE LAST PLACE I would expect to find Oliver Wendell Holmes is on Uncle's Income Tax material. But there he is: "Taxes are what we pay for civilized society."

Probably because I was deep in producing the FORUM, the idea jumped into my mind that this also applied to us in Al-Anon. No one likes to pay taxes; very likely we'd all avoid them if we could. But we do enjoy the civilized society which results from their payment.

So, to the Al-Anon application of this principle: given a free choice, I believe few among us would have chosen an alcoholic problem with which to live. Left to ourselves, we'd rather have had a tranquil life in sunny places. But what would it have been? Few of us are like Jack's beanstalk which sprang up miraculously. We have to grow, most of us slowly. And we can't grow without challenge.

By ourselves, most of us made a mess of our reactions and relationships. It took Al-Anon's teachings and philosophy to straighten us out; it took coping with our problem through the Al-Anon program to stretch us spiritually, make us understanding and accepting.

If that is the price we had to pay, the tax required to keep us from the moral death of smugness, then the civilized society we now have in our homes and hearts is worth it.

Problems Make Progress

PEOPLE WRITE Headquarters or the FORUM for help on problems, either personal or group. Sometimes they recognize these as growing pains and sometimes there is vast impatience that not all is perfect.

Happily the ones who do recognize unresolved conflict as a step in development already have won half their battle. That is, if they are willing to be unselfishly ready for whatever solution is best for all concerned.

To insist on one's own panacea, simply because it is one's own, often leads from conflict to open warfare.

Growing pains are part of normal development. Not all of us are conscious of physical growing pains but such conditions exist. We frequently do not recognize unhappy experiences or set-backs as spiritual growing pains. But pains or problems, if accepted rightly, do contribute to spiritual growth.

People who coast along, sliding through life without

allowing themselves to become involved in anything, seldom if ever develop great moral stamina.

It's about the same physically. Take my daughter for instance. When she was little, she had spent most of her life on a Montana ranch, in pure mountain air and glorious sunshine.

Then at four, we visited Chicago and Buffalo one winter. She immediately began a series of critical illnesses. I was wild. I stormed at the doctor, told him of her ideal background and could not understand why this had not protected her.

Naturally it hadn't, he told me. She'd never been exposed to anything and so had never built up any immunity against anything.

Thus, if you do have problems, personal or group, keep on writing us. We may be able to help. We'll surely try. But please remember that problems can make progress.

Words To Live By

IN A Chinese Fortune cooky I found the lines, "Fear of danger is ten thousand times more terrifying than danger itself."

Immediately I thought of myself in early Al-Anon days and of the hundreds of newcomers to our program who spend countless days and endless nights tortured by infinite fears.

I couldn't define them, exactly, nor can these newcomers. There never was time to think—I just spent it being afraid. Everything milled around in my mind until the line between sanity and insanity thinned to a thread, and a cob-webby one at that.

Fortunately for me the Serenity Prayer gave me my

answer. I could not ask for courage to change the things I could change unless I knew which things they were. I couldn't accept those I couldn't change, either, unless I had the wisdom to know the difference. And there was no wisdom in my uncontrolled spinning from one fear to another. I had to sort out and distinguish which was which.

In that process of sorting, I had to face my fears. From an instinctive pushing aside of something nebulous but horrible, something I'd rather not think about, I had to dig out and bring to light just exactly what kept me in chaos.

When I did this, I found the serenity (patches of it) which comes from acknowledging the worst. At absolute rock bottom, any place else is UP.

Once on the way up, I could help myself rise higher, just as I could allow myself to slip back. At that point "Just For Today" was invaluable: "Just for today I will not be afraid." Sometimes "Just for this minute I will not be afraid" got me by some bad spots.

Thus serenity grew and flourished.

Gradually I reached the point where I could realize that "Fear of danger is ten thousand times more terrifying then danger itself." I didn't put it in those words but they surely rang a bell for me when I read them recently. They are words to live by.

"Be Still, and Know That I Am God"

IT's SAID that many of us dig our graves with our teeth. I say that many of us make a hell for ourselves with our tongues.

We speak too quickly. When someone hurts us, we lash back. When it is life itself which hurts us, we fly apart. We're like dogs, chasing our tails, going nowhere fast, with each circle getting tighter. It takes almost a miracle to bring us back to reason.

Those of us living with the problem of alcoholism are fortunate because we do have a miracle to restore us to reason. We have guide-posts which already have helped thousands, to show us the way.

Ours is a program which demands thought. We have to weigh the past, learn from it, determine to benefit from it. We cannot do this successfully if we indulge ourselves in mental tantrums. We cannot do it all by ourselves. We need our fellow members and we need our Higher Power.

We know that the Higher Power has helped millions, is only waiting to help us. We are the break in the circuit, with our turmoil, our "alarums and excursions." Instead of frantically losing control when difficulties beset us, we should heed the psalmist: "Be still, and know that I am God."

Acceptance

WE IN AL-ANON are greatly blessed by the support we get from the Al-Anon program. From it we learn which things we can change, which things we must accept. We learn that a Higher Power is always at hand to ease our way. It is our privilege to spread the word of this philosophy not only to our children but to everyone with our problem.

My youth would surely have been less difficult had I been taught acceptance earlier. Nothing could change the fact that I followed immediately after a brilliant sister. I was not stupid, just average. But I came so close after my sister's shiny brains that teachers, accustomed to Mary's brilliance and expecting the same of me, put me down as mentally lazy. It infuriated me. I knew I was doing almost as well as I could and was being discounted.

One typical instance was our mutual French teacher. She cherished Mary's reply and broadcast it freely when the junior class was asked to define a gentleman. "One who acts, always, as if he were in the presence of God," said Mary without hesitation.

I, a freshman, recognized that definition as something pretty fine although then I'd have hesitated to talk so freely about God. I also recognized such an idea would never have crossed my mind.

But Mademoiselle vainly spent the next three years like a cat at a mousehole, waiting for me to come up with an equal gem.

Sixteen years of trailing after such clouds of glory left their mark on me. I rebelled and I resented. But I could not change the situation nor did I know enough to accept it.

Perhaps my stormy background accounts for my great reliance upon our prayer. One of Al-Anon's finest blessings and biggest helps is, "God grant me the Serenity to accept the things I cannot change, the Courage to change the things I can, and Wisdom to know the difference."

"As a Man Thinketh . . ."

IF YOU HAD a dollar for each time you've heard, "As a man thinketh, so is he," how far would they take you? I believe my dollars would take me clear to the Chinese Wall! There's something about thinking, however, which has no IF about it. Thinking can change one from a quivering mess of fear, a prey to every vagrant dread, into a well-adjusted, valuable person.

Many of us in Al-Anon fortunately have experienced such a change. And every one of us, even when new in Al-Anon, have seen it happen to others. Frequently the change came while a member was still living with an active alcoholic . . . and the only thing different about the situation was the mental attitude of the Al-Anoner.

No magic button will bring about this change, although the change itself is magical. It's accomplished through discipline, mental and spiritual.

It comes through a refusal to remain on the old treadmill of fear, worry and doubt. Actually it is a deliberate choice to put one's self into the hands of the Higher Power; to stop living in the unhappy past; to determine to "change the things we can."

Newcomers, perhaps, can accomplish only a moment of such positive thinking. But each moment is an entering wedge and the next one comes more easily. Added together, those precious moments soon become hours—days—and always. One's mind moves out of the squirrel-cage of worry on to an open road which leads out of difficulty . . . "As a man thinketh . . ."

Special Christmas Wishes

"Joy to the World," "Oh Come, All Ye Faithful," "The First Noel," no matter how many times we've heard these carols, they always bring a catch at the throat, a quiet, inner thrill. Something about the Christmas season makes every happiness happier. But that same something deepens sadness if we are troubled.

And, over the years, many of us have been troubled at

this season. Christmas cheer had been too cheery for our loved one and our house too filled with spirits instead of spirit. If you are among those in distress today, take heart. What if you have to be Father and Mother Christmas both? What if you, unaccustomedly, have to carve the Christmas turkey? Most of us have done it. And survived.

But, if you are in Al-Anon, you have hope. You know that alcoholism is a disease, not a disgrace. You know that AA has worked its miraculous change in well over 300,000 —why shouldn't it work for your partner? Even if AA is resisted now, it may not always be.

Should such a Christmas ever again come to our house, I believe I would say to myself, "I'll be like Scarlett O'Hara in Gone With the Wind—I'll worry about it tomorrow." And I hope I would detach myself enough from the turmoil so that some of the Christmas spirit would conquer the sadness.

I deeply hope none of us has a less-than-perfect Christmas. But if, unhappily, this is not true for all, my special Christmas thoughts and prayers will be with the troubled ones.

The Wonder of Al-Anon

HAVE YOU EVER marveled at the power of Al-Anon to attract and to hold persons of such varying backgrounds: ages, races, creeds and stations in life?

A very powerful religion frequently does this. But Al-Anon is not a religious organization. We do believe in a "Power greater than ourselves" but each of us may relate that greater power to whatever he chooses.

I find it natural to think of this greater power as God

and, through the appropriate Steps, have been able to come closer to Him and at times to sense His will for me.

But in various groups with which I have been associated, I have known others who were completely agnostic and some even were atheists. They had success with the program, too.

One substituted the group conscience as her greater power, another used "all outdoors" as more powerful, while a third thought of a Diesel locomotive as a higher power.

Although none of these concepts is religiously motivated, the three members holding to them could frequently give me glimpses into depths of the program which I had missed.

While Al-Anon is not a religious program, it definitely IS a spiritual one. We have no dogma nor doctrine to which we must subscribe. We are free to pick and choose what we wish from the various aids the program offers.

The emphasis is all spiritual in that it is centered upon discipline of self, upon self-improvement and growth, upon development of concern for others and practical ways to help them.

There is nothing in Al-Anon to shut anyone out—everything is centered on bringing people in. And the wonder of Al-Anon is that it keeps on doing just that: giving comfort, restoring confidence, and shedding light in dark places.

Each Day's Business

As I LOOK back, we children were very patient with our father. For such an old man (he was in his thirties and early forties) he knew an awful lot. He'd spend endless time taking us places we wanted to go, although they must have bored him stiff. So that it was only common politeness, when he occasionally philosophized, that we appeared to listen with respect—if not with understanding.

He was a doctor. As with all doctors, he occasionally met with death in his practice. It was at such times, I suppose, he used to say, "Never count on a deathbed repentance. The business of the dying is with dying. Live each day now, just as if it were your last and everything will take care of itself."

We were patient with such nonsense. We had to grow up to know what he was talking about. We had to grow up to know that probably he knew we'd have to, but that we'd remember. The particular bit about each day, and a lot of his other exhortations, I now recognize as simon-pure Al-Anon thinking.

EACH day is the ONLY day we have. And if there are things about ourselves we want to change, today is the day to change them, or at least to begin working on them.

If someone you know is in difficulties and a call would help, go pick up your phone: next week he might be in such deep sadness that you couldn't help then. A call today could lift him out of it.

If you have a debt of kindness to pay, pay it today, to the person to whom you owe it or to someone else in his place.

But do each day's business each day.

Loving Kindness

KINDNESS ISN'T ENOUGH—the Bible says we should show loving kindness. Yet how many of us do, habitually? Certainly we all rise to special occasions, when sympathy for someone shakes us out of our preoccupations, when illness occurs or disaster strikes.

But in our everyday associations, how well do we do?

How many times do we fly at the throat of our nearest and dearest for perhaps well-meant and well-deserved criticism of a friend, not a tenth as close to us as the one at whom we fly?

We're apt to call it being loyal, but real loyalty surely should be to those nearest and dearest.

Again, when we're tired and overwrought, do we let loose at the neighbors, our co-workers, or even upon utter strangers, or do we use the family as our safety-valve?

Perhaps you don't do those things. But, looking back, I know I have. It doesn't take a searching moral inventory to tell me that no stranger can ever be as exasperating as a close relative. But that is no excuse.

We are told we should be kind to one another. And the kind of kindness needed is loving-kindness.

Sharing in Al-Anon

FEW PERSONS, of themselves, are strong enough, wise enough, to spend years with an alcoholic problem without suffering marked personality changes. In spite of themselves, most become introverted, shy and distrustful of intimate contact with others.

Even after coming into Al-Anon, many of these people remain ill at ease and are afraid to talk in meetings, much less speak to groups. This is a great pity for they are missing the greatest blessing and the greatest help that Al-Anon can give. That is the gift of lightening another's load. As children we were taught it is more blessed to give than to receive. In Al-Anon we have opportunities for both and should train ourselves so that we can benefit from both.

In the beginning, at my very first Al-Anon meeting, a miracle happened to me: the burden of fear, superstition and shame which I had carried for years, was lifted by one of the speakers who could have been describing my life in her talk.

She gave me courage to change my thinking but it took months before I could talk to anyone about it. When I did gather up courage to do so, it was at an Open Meeting in Montclair, N.J. I found to my amazement that FOUR persons at that one meeting had carried my same load. That night they were released, as I had been, and got new courage, as I had.

It doesn't much matter where I talk—in the mid-west, in Prince Edward Island, here around New York or a few weeks ago in Washington to a large group of wonderful people—everywhere I go and every time I tell the miracle of my first meeting, I find that same miracle works for some one there.

Remembering the pit I had dug for myself, from which I had been lifted, I rejoice at spreading the word to another. I thank God for giving me courage to have told it the first time in Montclair. I learned that it's only the first time which is difficult and seemingly impossible.

This sharing of experience in Al-Anon is one of the greatest, most important parts of our program. I often wonder if we have any right to allow shyness, self-distrust or embarrassment to keep us from helping another, as I was helped? And as the dozens (I've lost track of the numbers by now) who carried my burden, were helped? It is frightening just the first time.

So, when there's an opportunity to share your experience, by all means do so. That's Al-Anon.

Looking at Lois

HAVE YOU EVER thought what you would most like to have said about you? I have. I don't spend my time in envy but I often think of something my husband said about Lois, one of the founders of our fellowship.

In Al-Anon's early days my nearest group was thirty miles away and held night meetings only. Jack had to go along to drive; since there was no AA meeting those nights, he attended ours. As sometimes happens, there were several meetings in a row which could have been dullish for an AA.

Driving up to the next meeting I said, "I'm sorry you're sort of trapped when meetings aren't interesting to you." He promptly remarked, "Never feel that. When I find my mind wandering, I just stop listening and look at Lois. I never tire of looking at her—her face shows so clearly how much she has put into life."

Then I remembered Lois' story: the early days of AA when their home was stuffed, from cellar to attic, with alcoholics in all stages of recovery; the long years of active work and travel with Bill as he went about the world on AA business; how, when AA first established its General Service Conference and Bill could relax a little, she had looked forward to relaxing with him. Not a chance.

On one of Bill's trips he had found many Family Groups and realized they needed some organization to foster their unity and growth. Who so logical and handy, as Lois, to do this fostering?

So, once again she was plunged into the middle of very hard work. But everyone who knows Lois also knows she didn't shirk, didn't even think of it as hard work, but as opportunity.

All this shines from her face—reflects how much she has "put into life."

When I am tempted to take an easy way out, refuse to do a job because I'd rather rest, I remember Jack looking at Lois, and I decide to give my own face a chance to show something besides closed eyes.

Wall or Bridge?

DID YOU EVER pass a field with a bunch of gophers sitting up like sentinels? The instant one saw or scented you, they all dove into their holes. Many of us in Al-Anon were just like those gophers.

At first we sat up and faced the world. But when something happened which we didn't like, we withdrew; we found a hole for ourselves and crawled in. Gradually, as unpleasantness followed unpleasantness, we increased our negative defense by building a wall about ourselves and the hole we hid in.

We overlooked or ignored the fact that we were making a bad situation infinitely worse. Actually our wall was not shutting out any unpleasantness. It was shutting unpleasantness in. It prevented other people from reaching us. It kept us in shadow instead of sunshine. It kept us turned in upon ourselves when we were far from being congenial company, even to ourselves.

No matter how we managed to reach Al-Anon under such adverse conditions, Al-Anon put a good-sized breach in that wall. We gathered courage to emerge momentarily through the breach, to grasp for Al-Anon's help. Gradually, through grasping for Al-Anon, we built a bridge out from behind our wall, out to other people, to normal living and to life. It was a bit shaky and infirm at first but as it grew stronger it became a two-way bridge from us to the world and from the world to us.

It seems madness to us now that once we chose to build a wall instead of a bridge. Because of the bridge we have built, we now can reach others who have not yet found the way.

Doors

WHAT'S ON THE other side of a door? Just think how many doors Al-Anon has opened for each of us!

The golden door—bright as a new day—which Al-Anon opens, is labeled Hope: hope for dreary creatures who too long have huddled outside in their own shackles.

That door to freedom was there all the time but we had held it shut tight, with resentment, self-pity and despair. We never gave a thought to what was beyond.

When we at last permitted Al-Anon to open the door of hope, we little realized the tremendous change it would make in our lives and in those around us.

We were content, at first, just to know we were no longer alone. It was a blessed relief to know others had worked through situations as desperate as ours. They showed that even where they had been slightly marred, they were not permanently damaged.

As we progressed, learned really to live our program, we underwent a change which, sooner or later, was noticed by our families.

Instead of keeping doors shut by bitterness, indignation and injured pride (a way which leads to madness) we learned to open them to understanding . . . understanding of ourselves and our mates.

Sometimes, even, because our Al-Anon door opened to

us, our partner sought the open door of AA. He saw the serenity we had gained through the Al-Anon program and wanted the help of AA for himself.

That bonus is not given to all of us. But working the program to the best of our ability does give us peace.

Al-Anon in Action

SUCH WONDERFUL THINGS happen in Al-Anon! Just a year ago we had a stupendous response to Ann Lander's mention of Al-Anon in her widely-read newspaper column. Her advice to a wife, concerned about her husband's excessive drinking, was to write Al-Anon Family Group Headquarters. That one brief mention brought in over six thousand cries for help. Who knows, perhaps some unhappy person is still keeping the article, trying to gather courage to write.

Then there is the request, recently received at the World Service Office, asking if the Chicago Alcoholic Treatment Center could reprint "Twenty Questions an Al-Anon May Ask Himself," from the June and July FORUMS. Naturally permission was given.

Who knows how far Marguerite G. A.'s questions will finally reach? Already they have spread from West Chester, Pa., via the FORUM, all over the world to our thousands of groups. And now that the Chicago Center is distributing them, those twenty questions may well bring countless hundreds more to seek Al-Anon's help.

Letters to the FORUM is another phase of Al-Anon which brings a similar glow to my heart. A note from Phyllis Q., of the Siuslaw Group, Florence, Oregon, reads: "I especially want to thank the FORUM for the saying, 'The only way to Push is with Prayer.' It rang a bell for me when I first read it and I use it many times every single day."

The FORUM can't take credit for anything but printing this item. Nearly two years ago, on page 6 of the November '61 FORUM, you'll find an item from Florence G., Wyandotte, Mich.:

"I've worked hard for our new group and feel frustrated when meetings remain small; I know, though, that as in so many other areas, the only way I can 'push' is with prayer."

Talk about casting a stone into the sea and spreading ripples to the ends of the earth—Al-Anon's a lot like that. Who knows when something you write may be the difference between despair and hope in another's life, ten thousand miles from you?

What real help are you keeping to yourself, when it might be working?

Al-Anon Gold

How LONG has it been since you've reread Al-Anon literature?

My face turned deep red recently when I got Helen B.'s (California's first WSC Delegate) letter in reply to my query about where I could find "Three Deadly Enemies." Because it had been several years since I'd read "Alcoholism The Family Disease," and because I'd always associated these enemies with the California tapes, I'd forgotten they'd been reprinted there.

Helen is far too fine a person to have answered, "How come you didn't know this?" She just sent me the mimeo'd sheet and mentioned in her note I could also find them in the pamphlet. She's quite a girl.

But naturally I did feel silly—and should have. It made

me wonder just what else I have been missing because I've let so much time go by without reviewing all our other booklets.

Al-Anon has a lot of literature. But people and groups are constantly clamoring for more. There'll be more. We have a splendid Literature Committee to produce it.

But is full use now made of what already exists? Or is it read once or twice and on to the next piece? Some part of one booklet may help in a given situation but months later, when that situation has changed, another part of that same piece may be a lifesaver in the new situation.

You would be well repaid by a thorough review of all our literature. It is full of golden nuggets. But gold is where you find it. To find it, you have to look.

"Fear Knocked at the Door—Faith Opened it"

ACCORDING TO ancient legend, The Plague went to Bagdad to kill five thousand people. Instead, fifty thousand died. When someone questioned him as to why he had slain so many, The Plague replied, "I killed five thousand, as I said I would. The others died of fright!"

Some of us are like those extra forty-five thousand. We don't actually kill ourselves from fright, but we do kill a lot of the best that is in us. We maim ourselves by fearing many things which just never happen.

By letting fear overwhelm us, we prevent ourselves from making sane and sensible plans to tackle life's problems.

Emerson says, "Do the thing you fear and the death of fear is certain." He doesn't say this is an easy thing to do. He doesn't say to wait a week, when you have more courage. He just says, "Do the thing you fear and the death of fear is certain."

If you fear heights, I doubt that Emerson would advise you to jump off a church steeple to overcome that fear. He'd be more apt to advise you to face up to your moral and spiritual fears: the inherent self-distrusts, shynesses and inhibitions which keep you from being your real self. Take his advice and remember: "Fear knocked at the door. Faith opened it. And lo! there was no one there!"

Vaya con Dios

CHRISTMAS BRINGS special joy, prompts us to a thanksgiving we may overlook at other times. We are favored beyond calculation because the gifts of Al-Anon are ours.

Think for a minute of the chances against us: there are 5,000,000 alcoholics in the United States. Figuring an average of only 5 persons associated with each, means there are 25,000,000 in need of Al-Anon help in this country alone!

Fast as our growth has been, we still probably have not reached more than 25,000 to 40,000 *in the whole world.* What did we few do to deserve this good fortune? Do we truly deserve it?

We do if we try to practice the program in all our affairs. When we do, I believe we are like Enoch who "walked with God." How better can we spend our days than in such company? No matter what we call our Higher Power, we cannot help but stretch ourselves spiritually if we are to accompany that Higher Power in all our waking hours.

To me, that Higher Power has always been God. I've never had difficulty in accepting God as the Supreme Being—my difficulty has been to keep myself free enough of the frets and strains of living so that I, too, may "walk with God."

That's why I love letters from Arbutus, our first WSD from Texas, who always closes even hurried notes with "Vaya con Dios." I'm devoid of Spanish but I'm sure it means "Go with God" and my spirits lift and I'm 6 inches taller.

So, for all Al-Anon, all Alateen and all AA, everywhere, may I wish for you every blessing of Christmas and may we all "Go with God" every day of the years to come.

Today's the Day

NEW YEAR'S DAY, traditionally, is the day when most of us aim to begin turning ourselves into soft-winged, haloed creatures of another world. That we seldom, if ever, accomplish this completely is beside the point. New Year's Day is a day of beginning and any beginning of self-improvement is better than continued complacency.

As a child, this day was always disappointing to me. I seemed never to learn from experience. Just as I expected some magic to show me the line between Illinois, where I lived, and Wisconsin, where I visited, I expected a difference between December 31st and January 1st.

But it was always just another day; Wisconsin wasn't pink, either, as it was on the map, with a straight black line separating it from an orange Illinois. I knew Illinois was green, really, with lawns, fields and woods, but Wisconsin should have been pink. So New Year's Day should have been different, too.

Now that I try to live by Al-Anon principles, with the 24-hours-at-a-time uppermost, I know that any day is a good day to begin work on whatever keeps me from practicing Al-Anon perfectly. It is not necessary to wait until the turn of the year to begin to turn over a new leaf.

The twentieth day of May or the tenth of March are just as good as January first—it's the beginning that counts.

But because something of childhood lingers in all of us, in spite of there being no real difference, January 1st is a good day to put our resolves into action, to concentrate more consciously on what we know we should be doing to improve the quality of our Al-Anon practice. If we should fail at first, there's nothing to prevent our beginning all over again, even on January second or February fifteenth. The main thing is to keep at it, never to be discouraged nor disheartened.

Happy beginnings to all of us and blessed accomplishments in the year ahead!

Try It Again!

THE HEADING on a leaflet I recently received startled me: "Try It Again" and I thought of my early days in Al-Anon. I believe I learned to walk early but, fully adult and then some, it took me more than three years to learn the First Step so that I really practiced it. I wasn't consciously trying to run things. I just thought there were things which hadn't been tried which would influence my husband.

Others have different problems: some, especially those working on the pamphlet "Just For Today," have difficulty in establishing a working time-table; procrastination dogs their feet.

Still others, highly organized and themselves proficient, determine to keep hands off while newcomers fumble through situations which seem simple to them and they intervene, even though they had determined to remain apart and let the newer one learn by doing.

Older members who have allowed themselves to dominate a group, may have decided to stand by on the sidelines, giving moral support, suddenly find themselves smack in the middle again, telling everyone what's what.

Discouraging, isn't it? Every time I stumbled on that First Step I thought I had it conquered. It was discouraging to have to pick myself up and begin again.

This all flashed through my mind as I read the heading, "Try It Again." And it seemed to me the most simon-pure Al-Anon admonition. It's the perfect sequel to "Why Not Try?"

No matter what your problem is, you'll never get anywhere with it until you try to overcome it, so "Why Not Try?" And if you don't succeed immediately, "Try It Again!"

A lot of us were brought up on the tale of Bruce and the Spider. If it takes seventy-times-seven, and more, to succeed in what we're aiming at, at least we are still alive to try the four hundred and ninety first time. Why not Try It Again?

Al-Anon's Second Wind

SECOND WIND suggests to most people great physical effort— a tired man running a long race, an exhausted horse plodding along extra, painful miles, or a swimmer tired seemingly beyond endurance, yet keeping on. That there is such a phenomenon is unquestioned.

There is, however, a second wind other than physical which we may not think of immediately. That is the spiritual second wind which keeps us coping with situations almost beyond tolerance.

We are about ready to give up when, from somewhere,

something keeps us going. This spiritual second wind is not automatic. We can count on it only if we condition ourselves for it.

Al-Anon, better than anything else, gives a kindergarten, an elementary-school and a university-course in such conditioning. Our whole program is based upon the idea of working on ourselves.

Every part of Al-Anon philosophy is pointed toward self-improvement. And every good experience in Al-Anon helps us appreciate that, through Al-Anon, we have had a spiritual awakening which gives us the obligation to help others as we have been helped.

When we are tempted to give up, to let chaos, turmoil and sadness overwhelm us, our background in Al-Anon steps forward and gives us our second wind to keep us going.

We may not know it is there within us. But in time of need we discover it. We find we have the strength, the will, even the wish to carry on to victory over ourselves.

That spiritual second wind Al-Anon gives us is its most priceless gift—worth all the blood, sweat and tears it takes to attain it.

"Nothing to Fear but Fear"

DO YOU SIT back at meetings, just listening, reluctant to give your opinion because you're shy? Do you hesitate to join the discussion because others seem to have better ideas to contribute?

If so, it's a pity. After all, similar as all our experiences have been, each learned a great deal from them and this knowledge really goes to work when it is shared.

The little extra twist you put on your interpretation of a Step or a slogan, might make just the difference in helping someone else understand it. Might make the difference between success and failure in his following that part.

Many of us come into Al-Anon not in complete control of ourselves. Either we are compulsively talkative or compulsively silent. Neither attitude is particularly good for the group, but the second is especially bad for the quiet one—no one knows quite how to help, because he doesn't know exactly where help is needed.

For your own sake try to contribute ideas and experiences. Begin in your own meeting and practice on the members. They aren't really a critical or formidable group, but just Al-Anon friends, there to help and be helped.

Then, when you're asked to talk elsewhere, don't draw in your horns, make excuses and refuse. That other group is just Al-Anon, too.

Speaking at meetings, large or small, is just 12th Step work on an extended basis. I believe if we all thought of it in this way and remembered that most of those in the audience are Al-Anons like ourselves, it wouldn't be difficult to get speakers.

There's a real challenge in speaking at meetings, especially large ones. There's also a tremendous thrill and reward.

A bit ago I spoke at the 5th Annual Al-Anon Rally in Detroit. I believe close to 700 were there. What did I have to give to so many different people? I have exactly what we all have—our own experience, and I gave my struggle with the First Step.

I'm sure no matter how hard I work on my talks, they are far from perfect. But they are honest, factual accounts of how I allowed a difficult experience to affect me, and how Al-Anon lifted me out of despair. No one else could give exactly that talk because no one else lived it and was affected by it.

And what a reward I had! Never was there a warmer, more generous welcome; never a more enthusiastic reception of an unknown out-of-towner; never did new friends seem like old friends so quickly. And this is always true.

So, if you are afraid to open your lips, remember that especially in Al-Anon, "We have nothing to fear but fear" when it comes to addressing meetings.

Stop! Look! Listen!

MOST OF TODAY'S roads are so built that old-fashioned level crossings of railway tracks are practically a thing of the past. And along with them have gone the Stop! Look! Listen! signs. I can't remember when I last saw one. Probably there are new, young members amongst us who've never seen one.

In a way that's too bad. We no longer need them with highways which cross railroad tracks on elevated bridges. But they would serve as valuable reminders for us to stop and think on certain occasions.

Too often, in impatient irritation, we sound off when it would be better if we stopped for even a moment's reflection.

If I seem to revert to this subject frequently, it's because so many of us do this so often. We seem opposed to learning better.

Naturally we can always admit regret when we do realize we've been wrong. But in the meantime we've set a chain reaction in motion—we have got ourselves upset; we have shown our displeasure, and because we did so as a result of too-hasty speech or of misunderstanding, the other person reacts adversely, and a mess results.

Probably all the unpleasantness could have been avoided had we not spoken so quickly—had we waited until we were thinking instead of speaking.

Stop! Look! Listen! signs, well distributed along all our mental paths and processes, might help all of us to calmer, friendlier, more peaceful lives. In winning friends and influencing people, they could be a decided asset.

If you've been having difficulty with others—naturally because *they* were wrong!—why not try a week of Stop! Look! and Listening, and see how much it helps.

Do It Now!

SOMETIMES IT TAKES a real jolt to shock us into an appreciation of just how important our twenty-four-hour program is. If we practiced it perfectly all the time, we'd act immediately on every good impulse we have. But all too often time presses at our heels and we move on to something else.

Such a shock came to me last week, with news of a Board member's husband's death. I'd always liked Jerry, especially after Adele told me he couldn't wait for the FORUM to come. He'd get home before she did, so he always read it first. She couldn't have it until he'd finished it.

One time, when I wrote a piece he particularly liked, he told her to kiss me for him. What editor could resist flattery like that?

I always planned to thank him personally for the nice things he said but we seldom met. When we did, very occasionally, it was at times like the Conference gathering at Lois's, or the picnic, where I'd be busy seeing people about the FORUM, and I'd think, "Next time I'll be more free and I'll stop then and really talk—thank him properly when I have time."

Now I have time. But Jerry isn't here to be thanked. Not that I believe he ever held neglect against me, or even thought of it. But it would be a comforting thought, since he is beyond me now, if I could remember having told him my delight in his appreciation of the FORUM.

Some good will come from all this, because I'll be more conscious of doing today's affairs today, of taking care of immediate concerns the moment the opportunity arises and not waiting for a better chance, which may not come.

Do it now is a good precept for me—and perhaps for you, also.

Understanding

PEOPLE ASK where ideas come from for the bits and pieces printed here. The answer is everywhere.

One piece I liked a lot came from the Income Tax form a year or so ago, where Oliver Wendell Holmes was quoted as saying, "Taxes are the price we pay for civilized society," and it made me think that living with an alcoholic was the price we paid for the really pricelsss gift of Al-Anon and we should see it in perspective.

Mystery stories have contained things which suggested ideas for many articles.

Since I read everything which comes within a mile of me, even matchbook covers, practically anything can suggest an article. July's comes from an Epilepsy Foundation stamp which read, "Understanding is half the treatment."

The French have a saying that "To understand all is to

forgive all," which always used to seem to come close to what our program does for us.

But now, thanks to the stamp, I believe "Understanding is half the treatment" really pinpoints it for us.

After years of trying unsuccessfully to take the First Step, and then finally making the goal, my resentment toward alcoholism finally waned. With that acomplishment behind me, there didn't seem any indication for "forgiveness."

With the First Step I knew the alcoholic was as powerless over alcohol as I, that it was a disease, so how did forgiveness enter? It seemed presumptuous to me even to think of it that way.

But understanding that it was a disease, a terrible compulsion beyond anything in normal comprehension, was the real beginning of my recovery. I don't know a single thing about the Epilepsy Foundation, except that they sent me stamps and I sent them a little money but I do know their slogan could well be Al-Anon's.

Why Are You in Al-Anon?

ARE YOU IN Al-Anon because someone said, "It's Al-Anon or else." Are you there to find a magic formula to dry up a consuming thirst? Are you there because life seemed too dusty to be worth while? Whatever the reason which drove you to seek help, you have found something in Al-Anon.

Even those who attend but one meeting get help, if nothing more than knowing others have had a like experience.

If you have stayed and have conscientiously worked the program, you have found a whole new way of life. This in spite of its being a "suggested" program only. No one tells you what to do. No one says you must do this to accomplish that.

Your own revulsion at your former attitude makes you reach eagerly for whatever it is which has made those others, with identical experience, so calm, serene and relaxed. You know that since they got it—and they show they have—you can get it too. All you have to do is to listen to them and learn.

One caution is necessary: Sir Winston Churchill has said it. He was a realist with the courage to say exactly what he meant. Remember when he told a desperate nation he could offer them nothing but "blood, sweat, tears and toil?"

He was equally realistic and uncompromising when he said, "It is no use saying, 'We are doing our best.' You have got to succeed in doing what is necessary."

We in Al-Anon have to succeed in doing what is necessary to regain our tranquility. We cannot be fair to ourselves, to our families, and to our responsibilities in life if we allow our problems—no matter how great nor how trying they are—to bog us down in a mess of quivering nerves.

If our best is not good enough, we have to concentrate on making it better. Help is ever-present in Al-Anon, even for the "loners," though that is the hard way to get it.

We fortunate ones in groups have an incomparably simpler time where we have successful examples always before us.

Let us never pause half-way with the false comfort of saying "We are doing our best." Let's dig in our heels, brace our shoulders and keep working until we have succeeded in doing what is necessary to become useful, attractive people again.

Don't Bury the Past too Deep

Lucy P. asked for my personal opinion on which is most helpful to an Al-Anon member: to try to close the door on the past or sometimes to look back on it?

If each of us is really the sum of his faults and virtues, the result of all his past, I personally don't believe we can ignore that past, just by waking up fresh each morning. That'd be fine but I don't see how it can be done.

If yesterday I stole a dollar from my neighbor, today I am a thief if I have not returned the money, acknowledged the theft and made amends.

But if I *have* made amends as far as is humanly possible, I do not have to live perpetually as yesterday's thief. I have made amends, can forgive myself and need to remember yesterday's fault only when tempted to commit the same error.

Most of us have done wrongs in the past at which we shudder, now that God has "restored us to sanity." Because I once hurled a priceless dish in a fit of uncontrolled anger, because I frequently yelled and screamed ugly, violent names and threats, I do not have to remember all of it in detail—go over it like a string of beads, each counting against me.

That was what I did then, when I knew no better and could do nothing else.

Now I do know better and I don't do those things. But since I have shoulder blades instead of wings, I am sometimes tempted to revert, and then it is well for me to remember that the past should teach me something. I did those things once; I cannot deny them.

I do not wish to repeat them. I can help prevent repetition by occasionally remembering how uncontroled I once was. I do not have to be the person I used to be and I do not have to allow the past to be a stone around my neck. After all, if I should sprout wings, it might impede their growth.

I just have to carry enough of the past along with me into my present so that it will help my future be fair and bright.

Something for You to Do!

THERE'S A LINE from the poet John Donne—the exact wording escapes me at the moment but the gist is, "I, a stranger and afraid, in a world I never made." That could be any of us. But we can't sit back and give up.

No generation of man ever is given the free choice of the problems which confront it; no individual ever really controls his future. He aims at it; he sometimes surmounts some difficulties. But there is always a residue, some flaw in himself or his surroundings, to cope with.

We in Al-Anon are fortunate that the flaw in our own surroundings is one which enables us to stretch out a helping hand, to give life-saving sanity to others now situated as we once were.

Had we not had the common background of alcoholism, we could never lead others to the acceptance we have gained.

God does not wait until we have attained perfection to use us for His purposes. He takes us as we are and enables us to share the serenity we have achieved with others who are still struggling.

The way is not always easy. I used to pass a gypsy fortune teller's studio with a sign in the window which read, "Come in and hear what you wish to hear." Always I used to think, "Wouldn't that be wonderful!"

But all the time I knew it was make-believe and the things which would help me to grow, and to mature (not just grow older) were things I *had* to hear . . . things like keeping hands off, living just one day at a time and allowing God's Will, not mine, to guide me.

If ever you are tempted to toss in the sponge and fall back upon the idea that it's "a world you never made," remember that of course you didn't make it but you don't have to leave it in the mess you found it.

You can't do much about many of the world's problems, but as long as there is one mate of one alcoholic in need of help, there's something for you to do. You've had a like experience, you have all of Al-Anon's tools—all you need do is use them, by sharing.

The Al-Anon Mail Bag

IF I COULD be granted just one wish for all Al-Anon, I think I might wish to have every member read one week's mail.

Naturally many letters are routine, taken for granted, like changes of address of secretaries. A lot is literature orders and notes enclosing contributions. But all show the Al-Anon spirit of helpfulness . . . groups keeping us posted so mail won't go astray.

I like to follow the literature orders mentally and think where they will eventually end up, and what power they will have to change lives. A piece sent to a group in New Mexico can well be forward-passed to South Africa!

I have written many times of the joy of speaking and the thrill which comes when my experience matches another's, and helps that person. This happened to me in Maryland a few weeks ago and makes that weekend an unforgettable one. When a woman in Detroit last spring said the most valuable part of my talk was when I said, detailing my efforts to control alcoholism before I took the First Step, "I did everything. The only thing I didn't do was do nothing." She'd been doing everything, too, but was going to do nothing from then on, except on herself. Delight, indeed!

But more rewarding even than that are the letters which come, desperate and frightened, asking for help and are followed a few months later with letters bubbling over with confidence and hope and thanks. Each of us in our group has had the same feelings when newcomers accept the program. This is a thrilling experience. But when it is multiplied a hundred times, through countless letters from all over the world, it catches at one's throat and softens one's heart.

Letters to the FORUM are especially precious because they all aim at helping someone. I wish I could print more. I wish most of all that all of you could read all of the mail—mine and Headquarters', both.

What's Wrong with Pollyanna?

HAVE YOU EVER gone through an entire day—granted you live among people and are not a reed, bending in the wilderness—without meeting one unhappy person? Or at least one person who *looked* as if he were unhappy?

Our little JUST FOR TODAY quotes Lincoln as saying that "Most folks are as happy as they make up their minds to be." So why shouldn't we make up our minds to be happy?

We're told (here I am not sure of my mathematics but I am of the idea) that it takes nineteen muscles to frown but only a dozen to smile. You'd think human inertia would make us smile more than frown. But few of us do.

"Just for today I will be happy." I'll make up my mind to be happy and then I shall be, along with Lincoln who went out of his way to lighten others' loads. If I have things to sadden me, and who hasn't, I'll think them over until I can find some good in them and I will not let them get me down.

One bus driver, who waits a moment for me to get aboard instead of slamming his door on my nose, one paper boy who smiles as he hands me my morning paper, can give me a lift for the day.

I can spread good will and good spirits by smiling as I hold a door open for the person behind me. If I smile, that person will smile back.

"Just for today I will be happy." If each of us plans this for each day of our lives, we'll see plenty of happy faces wherever we go and the blessings of the happy holiday season we all wish everyone will last far beyond Christmas and New Year's—we'll change our whole world. Christmas love to each of you.

Attitude of Gratitude

How MANY TIMES have you heard someone—usually a woman, widowed, with grown children or childless—say, "There's no one I have to please; no one I have to account to and no one to whom I owe anything. I can please myself."

But is this ever true? Certainly it is true of minor things—it doesn't matter if such a person chooses to eat on a tray instead of setting a formal place at a table. It is true it doesn't matter if she reads late and sleeps 'til nine o'clock.

If she had worn pastel colors all her married life when she really wanted bright ones, good for her if she goes out and buys fire-engine red shoes or a Kelly green dress. Surely both are harmless and quite satisfying.

It's this business of not owing anything to anyone which is impossible to justify. I do not believe it is reasonable that any person could reach mature years without owing something to someone—a kindness done, a thoughtful act in time of stress, a hope held out when things were dark.

I know that one can't continue to thank someone endlessly for a kindness done. But one can continue to be thankful that it was done and to look around for ways to express that thankfulness.

In our fellowship no one need look far to find someone still in need. Lifting that person's spirits with a thoughtful word or a kind act is a small payment on one's own debt.

Should you ever catch yourself saying, or thinking, "I owe nothing to anyone," stop and really think. Don't dwell on the bitter disappointments—concentrate on who and what helped you overcome them.

Don't count the hurts you have received but remember the kindnesses extended you—and repay them tenfold to anyone still in need. It is this ability to scatter blessings in recognition of blessings we ourselves have received, which makes us persons worth knowing and having as friends.

Be Generous with Your Past

LARGE NUMBERS of letters come to the FORUM, which is natural and good. Ten times the number would be heartily welcomed. But one thing is strange and it happens quite frequently: months or maybe years will pass without a single letter on a given subject. Then, out of the blue will come three, four or a dozen, from places as widely scattered as it is possible to be, all on the same subject.

In the past few weeks these multiple letters have been about fear of speaking to groups. This is something which concerns us all, because group meetings are an important part of our program. We need speakers for them, speakers who are willing to stand up and tell their own experiences, before and after the program.

Granted that some people are more shy than others, that it is difficult for them to address more than two people at once, that they prefer to remain in the background and do their share by washing cups or straightening up after meetings—both necessary jobs. Ask yourself if this is enough.

One of these recent letters shows a self-analysis which goes deeper than the others. This writer says she is, and always has been, afraid to speak in public. She pondered and came up with the reason that she was "afraid of making a fool of herself." Once she established that reason, she set to work to overcome that fear. Little by little she is training herself to talk to more people and I am sure it won't be long before she is addressing larger groups successfully. What has she got that you don't have?

I, myself, have as wild and silly a story as anyone possibly could have. I was so far gone I seriously asked a surgeon to break my husband's leg so he'd be immobilized and I could, Gorgon-like, keep him from going out after liquor. That doesn't show much sense—and I didn't have much—but my telling it has helped a lot of people feel they weren't too bad . . . they didn't slip back that far from the norm.

When one is seriously questioning his sanity, it is real

comfort to know that someone else, now apparently in full possession of himself, had gone farther off the rails than he, but still came back to sanity. How can anyone ever know this if no one speaks and says it?

There are a lot better speakers in Al-Anon than I am. But I am the only one who can tell *my* story. I am the only one who had my particular battle with the First Step. If some member still is having difficulty, after struggling six months with it, it is reassuring to hear that I fought four years to take it successfully. But I finally made it, and the whole program fell into place. Who else can tell them that? And if I do tell them, and someone in the audience is still fighting it, does it matter if I am not a silver-tongued orator? That person gets the message all right, and very likely his battle is cut short by months or perhaps a year.

My correspondent who analyzed her reluctance to speak in public as being caused by fear of making a fool of herself was very wise. I am sure it is fear of failure which ties her tongue. But why should she be afraid? We are all Al-Anons, one or five hundred of us. Each of us has a unique experience, enough like someone else's to help that person. But we have to share it. We have to tell it because it is our story and no one else can tell it.

Many people are helped just by looking around a group, seeing happy faces, and realizing members can laugh at themselves. But many more are given a tremendous lift when they hear a story like their own which ends successfully. But they have to hear it—they can't get it by osmosis. Don't let pride, fear or shyness keep it from them. Those three qualities are enemies of our program. Be generous with your past—someone needs it more than you!

"Time to Stand"

> A poor life this, if full of care
> We have no time to stand and stare.

W. H. Davies wrote that. I wish I had. I believe each of us has an extra moment in the day to flex spiritual muscles or to take a bit of time out.

I'm sure, no matter how busy each of us is, we could pause a minute and think of something wholly detached from ourselves, and we'd be better for it.

When one is living with an active alcoholic, all too often there are pressing financial problems. These are real and important. I have heard people say, *"I know alcoholism is an illness, but does my landlord? Will he wait?"* And all day and far into the night they are haunted by the thought of what they will do for the rent.

Still others slog through each day, trying to do the impossible of keeping up with a family and a house which is too much for one alone. All day they say to themselves, "As soon as I wash the clothes I'll scrub the kitchen but when can I get at last week's darning?"

They are all so oppressed by the burden of the moment, real as it is, they never get a second's refreshment. Handicapped by a serious problem to begin with, that problem is soon aggravated out of all proportion.

It would be better, instead of eternally running on this vicious treadmill, if one pulled himself up short and said:

"Look, now, that is enough nonsense for a while. Put every worry out of your cluttered mind and think for two minutes of the nicest thing that ever happened to you—or of the most peaceful place you've ever been."

Don't allow yourself to get trapped into self-pity that the nice thing isn't happening now, nor that you aren't in that peaceful place. Just live it over again and relax in it.

There's little that is new in this idea. But it does have authority behind it. Nearly two thousand years ago when Christ walked the earth, He dropped in to see two sisters. One sat and drank up His wisdom and inspiration. The other scurried from pot to pan, hastened to tidy up for Him and got herself in a stew so that she soon complained to Him that Mary just sat and listened and left all the work to her.

He listened and agreed. But, He said, "Mary has chosen the better part and it shall not be taken from her." After all, He was the first to say that man did not live by bread alone and He put spiritual things first.

Nobody knows better than I that the hours of the day and the night are not made of rubber. But as I walk along a city street, I *can* look up and see a jet streak across the sky; I can pause a second and watch a flock of pigeons swoop and wheel, just for the joy of movement.

If I'm on a crowded bus, I can think myself back to a Montana meadow strewn with a million wild flowers. I can see whole ranges of glorious mountains, the white-on-white of their rugged snowcapped crests sharp against the clouds behind them. I can reflect that those mountains were there before a man lived to see them.

Instead of the squirrel cage I used to spin in, I now take time to stand and stare. And I'm happier and better for it.

Testimonial to March's "Time to Stand"

As everyone well knows who has ever heard me speak, who has read more than ten lines I have written, and who has talked five minutes with me about Al-Anon, I had the greatest difficulty with the First Step. When I finally was able to accept it, the whole program fell into place and I have since tried to practice it in all my daily affairs.

I had a real test recently of practicing what I preach—although I do hope I don't sound preachy.

Just as I was finishing up the March FORUM at the end of January, I had a most horrifying experience. In elegant New Yorkese, I was "mugged" by two young men in the lobby of my building, shortly after six in the evening.

One held me, helpless, while the other snatched my handbag. My right middle finger was broken. Pain and shock later made sleep a bit difficult.

That first night I did take a capsule the doctor prescribed but my mental state was such that the medicine couldn't relax me. Every time I closed my eyes I felt that arm come from behind, crushing my mouth and holding me helpless. I'd shiver and shake and get the horrors. If ever anyone was on a vicious treadmill, I was. Then I suddenly remembered a "Time to Stand" I'd written so recently.

My first thought was, "you certainly are a dandy to give help to anybody. Why don't you take your own advice?"

Within moments, I felt myself back in Montana in the springtime with my daughter. We'd have to watch where we put our feet as we crossed meadows and pastures, so that we'd step on the fewest wild flowers. There were so many millions of them we felt free to pick some. So I set myself mentally to gathering Mariposa lilies, fritillarias, moccasin flowers, lady-slippers and countless others. I still couldn't sleep but I could relax and did.

Every time the thought of that terrifying experience tried to creep back into my mind I instantly thought of Montana's peace and quiet—either the dramatic springs, the satisfying summers or the marvelous winters with mile upon mile of spotless snow.

In a week's time, the awful thoughts stopped coming while I was conscious. And it has been two weeks since I woke my husband up by screaming in my sleep—I'm working on my subconscious now and having some success, apparently.

I don't recommend going through such an experience to prove a point—even one of my own—and the things I've suggested before have always been ones I'd already tried and proved successful.

But the fear and anxiety I'd known previously were child's play to the horror and terror, the physical indignity and all the rest incidental to this mugging. What worked in such circumstances will work in others equally serious.

There's nothing like taking time to "stand and stare."

In the Presence of God

A MOST IMPORTANT part of our program reminds us that we have only today with which to concern ourselves . . . only right now, in fact.

For many of us, blotting out the past is a tremendous comfort. We are not proud of past performances; we know we sometimes were tried beyond endurance but also know we let off steam many times on the nearest person, frequently on our children who had done nothing to deserve the wrath poured out on them.

If we did no lasting harm to them, and fortunately few of us did, it was because they instinctively knew we were not really ourselves, and thus bore no malice. They came out of the ugly picture better than we.

Blotting out the past is good; it is healthy not to brood over it. But enough of it should be remembered to prevent us from ever falling into the same error again.

I've written this incident before but you can see the

impression it made on me. When we were very young, my older sister had her own definition of a gentleman: one who acts always as if he were in the presence of God.

That's quite a definition for a sixteen-year-old to think up herself and I've never forgotten it. I believe most of us want to consider ourselves ladies and gentlemen. If we live by Mary's definition, we'll have no occasion ever to be sorry for the things we do.

If God were visibly present, I cannot imagine any of us venting impatience on innocent heads. It is hard to imagine any impatience at all in such a Presence.

Thus, when trials come (and what life is without some?), Mary's definition is a sheet anchor, and I gladly share it now with anyone in need.

"This Is the Day—"

"THIS IS THE DAY which the Lord hath made." The psalm is one of thanksgiving and while it indicates difficulties and enemies, they are already vanquished and the general theme is of rejoicing.

All too often we quote this line on bright, perfect days, when everything is going well for us. We feel it goes with such days, but how about dark, troubled ones? God made those days too—in fact He makes all days and has been doing it for a long time so there's little that's accidental about them.

If we could learn to accept trials, setbacks, and disappointments as part of the days that God hath made, we'd begin to gain perspective.

We know nothing is going to last forever. We know we must have something to overcome, to pit ourselves against, if we are to grow and become strong. We don't develop character licking marshmallows.

When we learn to take the bad, as well as the good, in stride, then we have begun to mature, to become persons worth having for friends, ones upon whom others can count.

Those who are a mile in the air today, and sunk in the depths tomorrow, are not much good to themselves nor to anyone else.

It's not written anywhere that just good things should happen to us. We need checks, restraints and postponements, as well as rewards and satisfactions.

Let's recognize that today—and every day—is the day that God hath made and derive some good from it, rejoicing.

Joy in Al-Anon

IN THE PAST few weeks, as this is written, several hundred letters have come to Headquarters in response to a mention of Al-Anon in a syndicated article. It was my privilege to handle 60 or 70 of these letters because I can again be a regular volunteer at the World Service Office.

Things are different there now. Twelve years ago, before my USO job, when cries for help came we were delighted to be able to refer inquirers to groups a hundred miles or more away. All-too-often groups were five hundred miles away and all help had to be given by correspondence.

It was a joyful surprise, when I counted up and found that more than half the inquiries came from persons in towns where an Al-Anon group was already established. Of the balance, most came from persons within forty miles of a group, and with today's transportation, that is not a hopeless distance. What a joy to tell those people how near at hand there was personal help for them!

And in that same period a letter came from Horicon, Wis., saying their group had had growing pains, problems, etc., and had dropped from a large group to only two. Those two, however, had kept on with regular meetings, reading and discussing Al-Anon topics. To their delight two new members had just joined them, overwhelmed with gratitude for finding help.

Marie wrote: "I felt like crying but held the tears back as I knew I must give them understanding, not sympathy. How very important it is to remember that even if a group dwindles to just a few members, those members should not give up. I thank God that Betty and I decided to keep a light burning lest a troubled person was seeking what we had been privileged to find."

Thank God for such a spirit in keeping a group alive, and thank God for all the other groups for being there to reach out a helping hand to those in need. We are indeed blessed.

Sermons in Stones

JUST A WEEK AGO, at noontime, one of our group telephoned me to say it was impossible for the one who was to lead the meeting to be present. Would I pinch-hit?

I am a newcomer to the group because it is a daytime meeting and while I was working I could not attend. Of course I accepted. Since there hadn't been a Tradition meeting in the months of my attendance, I read them and very lightly outlined what they meant to me. This was well received.

Then, as it is a discussion group, I asked if there were any newcomers or anyone who wished to talk about anything. One woman spoke up and said she was desperate, was thinking of leaving her husband or doing something drastic to herself. We told her we could give no marital counseling but we did give her a resumé of our own experience.

Everything we suggested that had worked for us was countered with the flat statement that her case was different or she'd already tried it. It was sort of a hopeless situation because her mind was tight shut, yet she obviously needed help desperately.

I went home rather depressed, the meeting a stone in my heart. I felt I'd led the meeting and should have found some acceptable answer for her.

My husband came home and sensed my worry, so I told him of having failed completely to reach a woman and that it bothered me because I had chaired the meeting. Naturally I said only that a woman had come for help and had not got it, although every person there had tried her best to give it.

He thought a minute and then said, "You shouldn't let it get you down. Something that was said may reach her later. And even if it doesn't, you said every member of the group tried to help and did their best. It's tough you couldn't reach her but the meeting wasn't wasted: every member there benefited from trying."

Then Shakespeare's lines from "As You Like It" popped into my head:

> *Sweet are the uses of adversity;*
> *Which, like the toad, ugly and venomous,*
> *Wears yet a precious jewel in his head;*
> *And this our life, exempt from public haunt,*
> *Finds tongues in trees, books in the running brooks,*
> *Sermons in stones, and good in every thing.*

That meeting *was* a stone to me but there *was* good in it, although, in my disappointment, it had to be pointed out to me.

A Bug's and a Bird's Eye View

IF WE TAKE a good look at what Al-Anon has done for us, most of us see that we, personally, have gained greatly. From gibbering, hagridden, craven cowards, a close look at ourselves shows we've gained courage, confidence and a more-or-less-great measure of serenity.

That is quite an impressive accomplishment for a program, itself purely voluntary and suggested, to achieve. It is one which has no do's or don't's in it, other than keeping an open mind. It leaves acceptance wholly to each individual.

Any program which accomplishes this can stand on the record alone. But take a moment to think, how much *more* Al-Anon does. Good wrought in its members never stops there. It spreads far and wide into all personal relationships, to the families and to the community.

When a frightened, insecure, immature person really accepts what Al-Anon can give, when he faithfully practices the program in all his daily affairs, that person stops holding himself as the exact center of the universe. He stops fighting battles which are not his to fight. He concentrates on actions where he has a chance to win. He relaxes enough so that he can again think of others and can again make a normal contribution to his home, church and community.

No outsider ever can say which home should be broken and which should stand. But Al-Anon has saved many and many a home from being broken.

Al-Anon has helped countless children regain respect for

their alcoholic parent, not only through teaching that alcoholism is a disease but by the changed attitude of the non-alcoholic. It has prevented numberless children from ever losing this respect through the same teaching.

It has changed many a home from a cat-and-dog kennel back to a home where there is acceptance, compassion and love.

So, if ever you become discouraged by a bug's eye view of your own progress in Al-Anon, be patient with yourself. Try a little harder. Remember what you were in pre-Al-Anon days. Countless others before you have freed themselves of daily, mundane failure in understanding, have risen above all of it, to get a bird's eye view of ultimate success.

What has been done, *you* can do. And it's worth the unhappiness along the way. After all, how many people can change themselves from cowering wrecks into valuable citizens? Through Al-Anon, you can.

Alice and Al-Anon

AL-ANON MEETINGS frequently remind me of The Mad Tea Party. They are very like and very different: "You should say what you mean," the March Hare said to Alice.

"I do," Alice hastily replied; "at least—at least I mean what I say—that's the same thing, you know."

"Not the same thing a bit!", said the Hatter, "Why, you might just as well say that 'I see what I eat' is the same thing as 'I eat what I see!' "

"You might just as well say," added the March Hare. "that 'I like what I get' is the same thing as 'I get what I like!' "

Many Al-Anon members are living with a still active

problem of alcoholism, which is not like Alice's Wonderland but certainly is just as topsy-turvy. In my own group I believe more than half the membership is numbered here. But, like Alice, they are trying to understand and make themselves understood under difficult circumstances.

The greatest and the most rewarding thing of our meetings is that we meet with a *willingness* to understand. No one barks at us "to say what we mean" if we have phrased something badly. Members take time and trouble to sort out the underlying meaning.

Best of all, our meetings are a place where we can say anything about anything which is troubling us, without having to wonder three times if it will touch off an adverse reaction. That is of priceless value to anyone living with a nervous, resentful partner still fighting a violent battle within himself.

When a situation resolves itself, as it usually does sooner or later when real serenity is attained, this freedom of speech is not as essential as in the early days. But it is always welcome. Some newcomers never say anything at all for months on end. But all the time they are absorbing the relaxed atmosphere and benefiting from it.

Infrequently, someone leaves a meeting not-too-happy about something which has been said. Even this is not all bad; it stimulates reflection, not on what was said, but on what was meant or what was accomplished at the meeting. And a better understanding ensues.

Due reflection on a program based on loving-kindness, a desire to learn and to understand and to help, deepens our appreciation of Al-Anon. It makes us work at meaning what we say and saying what we mean, and everybody gains.

All That's Needed

SOMETIMES SITUATIONS arise when I am helpless and I say, "All I can do is pray." That sounds apologetic and I am not, at all. I feel I am extremely fortunate that I can pray. For me, the Higher Power is God, my Father in Heaven.

I know there are others whom I consider less favored than I who do not so believe. In Al-Anon, however, they do have a Power greater than themselves which helps them through rough spots. None of us are alone anymore.

But I came on something recently in Pat O'Brien's WIND AT MY BACK, where he tells of a serious illness of their eldest child. His wife worked endlessly at her bedside and suddenly, miraculously, the child became better. His wife sought him and found him praying: "There was nothing else I could do," he told her.

"Nothing else was needed," she answered him.

There was my answer: I hope I never again say, "All I can do is pray." If there is something else to do, I'll do it and pray that I'm doing right. If things are out of my hands, I'll say, "I'll pray."

To me, prayer is a reaching, a stretching of myself, an earnest effort to become closer to God.

I feel that others who do not believe in God as I do have something which helps them—a member of a group I once belonged to felt her Higher Power was the group spirit and it never let her down; she practiced beautiful Al-Anon with this concept.

Because I write the FORUM some members think I know more Al-Anon than they do, that I have better answers. I wish that were true but I well know it is not.

Every one of us constantly learns from everyone else. Every one of us has some part of the program which means more to him than any other and which he understands better. But we all have a Higher Power on which we can surely rely.

Our 24-Hour Program

A WOMAN returned to our group after an absence of eight months. Something had happened which annoyed her and she heard herself making completely uninhibited charges which shocked her—but she kept on.

At the end of the scene she sort of came to and thought "I'd better get back to Al-Anon." Our meeting was on the Tenth Step, "Continued to take personal inventory and when we were wrong promptly admitted it."

This woman reminded me of myself in pre-Al-Anon days. I have visual proof and a powerful reminder of the Tenth Step: our china is Spode which we use for everything because of lack of cupboard space. The set came to me intact after my mother's death.

One night I got upset because things looked like the start of a binge and my husband came into the kitchen and harped on something which looked important in his confused state. A few minutes of this were enough to inflame me.

Ordinarily, self-control is my major pride; I can't abide loss of it in anyone, child or adult. That night I became so irritated I couldn't hang on to myself. I knew I should control myself but I didn't care. My eye lit on the dinner plates: I grabbed one, raised it high above my head and crashed it to the floor!

Even as I did it, watching myself in horror, I thought "This pattern is open stock. I can replace the plate." But

Mother had been dead ten years by then and it was no longer open stock, and I have never been able to get another.

Thus for all the years between, that plate I deliberately smashed and the scene I created always come to mind when I see the pile of plates. In the 20 years since then other plates have been broken and I've forgotten how. But I cannot forget that one—it's a constant reminder of how I once was and how much worse I'd be today without Al-Anon. Uncontrol, I believe, is also a progressive disease.

Thank God for Al-Anon; without it I might now have been tossing the whole set, and aiming not at the floor but at whoever or whatever was irritating me.

Al-Anon's is a twenty-four hour program. To many people this phrase means that we have only today in which to face our problems. It means that to me.

But it also means that we have to practice the program every minute of every twenty-four hours. We cannot swallow the program whole; we cannot leave it behind us in our meeting room. We have to take the Steps one at a time and make them our own, give them enough quiet thought so they are an integral part of ourselves—not something we take up and put down when we feel like "letting go."

Perhaps I am the only one in the world to whom a dinner plate "which isn't there" is a perpetual reminder of the Tenth Step. But it is certainly an effective one for me. Perhaps without Al-Anon and its self-discipline I'd never have been able to meet many difficult situations—for life itself presents constant problems. Al-Anon helps us meet them with courage and control.

The Person I'd Like to Be

SOMEWHERE in the glut of my indiscriminate reading, I picked up the idea that each man walks triply: the man he was, the man he is and the man he would like to be.

As all roads once led to Rome, after many years in Al-Anon, practically any new idea I meet quickly leads to consideration of it in terms of Al-Anon thinking. This concept of a triple-man appeared to me to be a *natural* Al-Anon idea.

Each of us knows the person he was, if we give it a little thought. If we are willing to be objective, each of us knows the person we are.

If we have been unhappy enough with the person we were, we have worked to change that person into one more suited to our ideals. We probably have not accomplished all the changes we desire, but we do get occasional glimpses of the person we'd like to be.

I do not know any Al-Anon member who was perfect to begin with, nor one who is perfect now. I do know numbers of them who have allowed anxiety, resentment and unhappiness to warp them, who have lost bright, sunny dispositions.

In this phase the person they were had become complicated by the person they are, and the unhappiness and discontent fortunately has driven them to Al-Anon, which, if they will work at it, will help them to become the person they would like to be.

For a guide to this end I can think of none better than the Prayer for the Day printed on the back of our little pamphlet "Just For Today" which sums it all up in the last lines:

"For it is in giving that we receive; it is in pardoning

that we are pardoned; and it is in dying that we are born to eternal life." To me, those are words to live by—ones I'd like never to forget as influences in making me the person I'd like to be.

The Wisdom of the Serpent

SERPENTS, to whom unusual wisdom is widely ascribed, have never been particularly appealing creatures. But I am indebted to one for a thought which comes to me often. He is G. B. Shaw's Serpent in "In The Beginning," who says to Eve, "You see things and you say 'Why?' But I dream things that never were; and I say, 'Why not?' "

Frequently I think of this at our weekly meetings when newcomers are present. Their burdens, their loneliness, their fears and resentments are so great that almost all they can say is "Why?" "Why did this happen to ME?" is implied if not said outright.

They know their own unhappy experience and find it difficult to believe that little or nothing of what they can tell is new or startling to the group. They do sense that the group has had help from something; there is an unmistakable atmosphere of acceptance and serenity which they feel and which usually makes them return to learn how to achieve it themselves.

More than half of our group are living with active problems, mates who have not yet accepted help or not even acknowledged they have a problem.

But Al-Anon's program has been of such help to the members that they can and do look forward to the day when things will straighten out. They can dream of this day which has not yet been and say to themselves, "Why not to us?" and they take heart.

It seems strange that all-too-often people find it easier to believe bad news than good. If they are unhappy, they dwell on that unhappiness, rather than look to a change.

So, to all those who see things and say "Why?" let Al-Anon show you how to dream things that never were and say to yourselves, "These things can come to me. Why not?"

Looking for God

". . . ONCE, from an interest in the history of mathematics, I was led into Blaise Pascal's *pensees;* he said that when you start looking for God, you have already found Him."

That, my friends, came not from inspirational reading but from one of my beloved mystery stories. Imagine! Gold *is* where you find it.

The above quotation contains a most moving thought. All too often, especially with newcomers to our program, one hears someone say, "I used to believe in God but through my difficulties I grew away from Him and no longer believed."

I do not think these people ever had lost God. They had mislaid their contact with Him for a time but He was there, waiting patiently, for Al-Anon to restore communication. Imagine the humility of God, waiting for *us*.

There are some people, however, who never had any belief to lose. But through Al-Anon, or some desperate experience previous to it, they, also, found God.

All through the Steps and Traditions there is constant mention of a Power Greater than ourselves, of our Higher Power and of God, even "God as we understand Him." Naturally this repetition starts something in their minds, when they see how it has served to help others. They, too, "come to believe."

Thus, for any who are still in that arid, unhappy desert where you feel yourself alone but sense there must be something else, remember: *there is*. Once you start looking for God, you have already found Him. He is there, simply waiting for you to call upon Him.

Remember also, we have been told, "Ask and ye shall receive. Knock and it shall be opened to you." Does it take much courage to ask? Since He has helped so many before you, is it difficult to believe that He will help you?

"Once you start looking for God, you have already found Him."

Ripening or Rotting?

As a child there were some of our family friends whom I instinctively avoided as much as I could. They were harsh, inflexible, and never laughed. Others drew me like magnets and I could spend endless hours with them, despite the gap in ages.

Later, as I grew up, I learned that tragic unhappiness had come to both sets. It used to bother me that one person had become so bitter and withdrawn that it was agony to be with him, while another, with equal cause, reached out a hand in friendship and welcome.

I was very fortunate in my parents, and in being one of eight children. No two people, with adult responsibilities, have time to spoil eight children. But they always had time to soften blows which come to all children, and to make us understand what was important and what wasn't.

Above all, they taught us we had a place in life and work

to do in it—that this was our work and no one could do it for us. We had responsibility as human beings, responsibility which increased as we grew older.

So I grew up, normally and happily, and was outgoing and seemingly well adjusted. But then came years of living with a problem too big for me, in ignorance, and alone.

The day came when I realized I was becoming one of the bitter, resentful people I'd avoided as a child. I had long since divided all adults into two classes; those who ripened and mellowed as they grew older, and those who simply rotted.

Unmistakably, I could see that I was rotting instead of ripening. But until Al-Anon showed me how to change I was helpless. I prayed for serenity, courage and wisdom. Gradually I improved. If I have not completely cured the rotting, I have at least arrested the tendency, and my everlasting thanks go to Al-Anon for what mellowing I have attained.

A Twenty-four Hour Program

DR. RUTH FOX has worked for many years with alcoholics. She has a deep understanding of them. I remember her telling of one patient who had had the greatest difficulty with the AA program. She listened and asked, "How long since you've been to a closed meeting?" He said he didn't care for closed meetings and never went, only to open ones.

"There's your trouble," she said. "Closed meetings are where you get the real AA program—where you get down to the brass tacks of it. Open meetings are the frosting on the cake."

Naturally I've never attended a closed AA meeting. I don't belong at one. But I'm sure I know what Dr. Fox meant.

Our Al-Anon speaker meetings are splendid and there's a lot to be learned by listening to other people's stories. But I believe there's more to be learned from a round-table discussion of the principles of the Al-Anon program.

When a speaker tells his story, it may or may not jibe with your own experience and thus may not be helpful. When you are having difficulty with any part of the program and ask for help on it, the whole group in a discussion meeting offers its best thinking on that one part alone and you are bound to be enlightened.

Those members who avoid meetings on the Steps or Traditions, and attend mostly the speaker meetings, I believe, show a lesser grasp of the program. They are attentive and listen well, it is true. But Al-Anon is a "sometime thing" with them, not a twenty-four-hour program. They are apt to leave the program behind them in the meeting room, not practice it in all their daily affairs.

It is only, I believe, when something happens which makes them put the whole program into practice, which makes them work at all phases of it, that they gain the very real help of Al-Anon.

When Evil Triumphs

SOMEWHAT SHORT of two hundred years ago Edmund Burke said, "All that is necessary for the triumph of evil is that good men do nothing." This comes to mind every time people write to say that their group is dying because one "Mrs. Al-Anon" will not give up . . . she feels it is her group and she must remain in authority.

To begin with, no one person in all Al-Anon has authority over a group or another Al-Anon member. "Our common welfare comes first." The First Tradition does not go on to say, "it comes first, last and always," but that's the way true Al-Anon works.

These correspondents with Mrs. Al-Anon-trouble always sound confused and very troubled. Naturally, it's a tremendously important problem and if they'd found the answer they wouldn't have written. But also they usually sound as if they'd done little to improve the situation—a bit as if they'd been Burke's good men who did nothing so that evil was flourishing.

What is there for them to do? First, I believe, an honest recognition of the situation calls for tremendous courage, a determination that the situation must be changed. In order to achieve this goal they must harden themselves to see it through, regardless of personalities, and not stop at the first setback.

I believe they can do nothing by talking among themselves and permitting it to continue. Rather, a few, two or three, should take the onerous and disagreeable task upon themselves of drawing up a blueprint of the group, pointing out what has happened to it—members dropping out, undercurrents, etc.—and privately presenting it to the overzealous chairman. I believe they should draw up By-Laws, group guides or whatever they want to call them, and see to it that they are not only adopted but followed. I believe that if the misguided chairman practices Al-Anon, she may temporarily be hurt and resentful but eventually she will see the light and will return.

But in this, as in many other situations, "all that is necessary for the triumph of evil is that good men do nothing."

Living by Glimpses

IF YOU REALLY apply the Twelve Steps of Al-Anon, every minute of every day offers an opportunity to put them into practice.

Acoustics are bad in my church. I have to strain to hear the sermon. Most times I get only a phrase here and there, so perhaps it's easy to understand why my thoughts wander. Just the other day a phrase got through to me, out of the jumble. My instant thought was, "That's pure Al-Anon."

What I heard was, "Doing good . . . silence ignorance. Live as freemen." In Al-Anon, "carry the message" and "restore us to sanity." The rest of the sermon time I spent correlating these words with the Twelve Steps and perhaps sermonized myself. At any rate, I somehow caught a glimpse at what living our program fully could mean.

Many times such glimpses come: as yesterday, when a car, entering a garage well in front of me, blocked the sidewalk. I was annoyed because I did not want to go into the street, into traffic, to get around it. I was saying pithy things to myself as I approached the stopped car. Just as my blood boiled and as I got within ten feet of it, the car smoothly rolled out of my way, leaving the walk clear. That time, the "24 hour program" jumped to mind but I sheepishly said to myself, "For you, it should be 24 minutes or 24 seconds."

Living by glimpses, such as these, is really what we do in the Twelfth Step when we "practice the program in all our daily affairs." When we do that we really are making the program work for us and us for it.

The Up-Hill Road

THE BEST PART of Al-Anon, as I see it, is that it teaches us to be realistic, to accept the fact that there are things we cannot change, things we can, and encourages us to distinguish which is which.

No one says it is fun to live with alcoholism, especially when the problem is acute. It is not fun for the alcoholic, either, as far as that goes. But Al-Anon and AA are the two greatest guides on coping with the situation that have yet been devised.

Each of us has his own limit of tolerance. When that point is reached, the fortunate one among us, through Al-Anon's teachings, finds the courage to face his life as it is, to stop milling around in a welter of fears, frustrations and nightmares. When things have got as bad as they can get, there's no way to go but up.

Al-Anon does not say it will cure the problems besetting us. But it will, and does, help us to live more equably with them. It does not say, "Do this, and your problems are over." Nor does it say that even if you do all it teaches, you'll never have another problem. In a wide reading experience I've never found a seventy year, or even a six month guarantee for a completely happy, problem-free life.

What Al-Anon does is to stiffen our minds and our wills to accept what comes, to get good out of everything by seeing that each experience makes for spiritual growth. Christina Rossetti expressed this acceptance in fewer words than I: "Does the road wind up-hill all the way? Yes, to the very end. Will the day's journey take the whole long day? From morn to night, my friend." This is truly realism and true acceptance of that realism.

Our up-hill road is frequently a very difficult one. But it does lead to a beautiful view if we remain faithful to Al-Anon's guideposts.

Do You Pass the Buck?

DURING WW II we spent nearly two years at an air base in Nebraska before Jack, my husband, went to the Orient. One of our great friends was the Quartermaster Captain. Jack always said he was the best QM. he'd ever met; most of them, in his long military experience, doled out supplies grudgingly, as if they were personal property. Captain Roberts issued them cheerfully.

The thing which first impressed *me* with him was the sign he had over his office: "The Buck Stops Here." In the service it's nice to know it does stop, and where.

Many times at meetings I remember Captain Roberts and his sign. I attend a daytime discussion group where many newcomers come for a time and then leave to join groups nearer their homes. Usually they are women living with an active problem; it's their first contact with Al-Anon and they are decidedly in need of help.

The first thing which impressed me when I was new to the group, and it still impresses me, is the fact that every member speaks up when she is able to help the newcomer. This was not always true of other groups of which I was a member. Usually there were two or three who seldom said anything beyond joining in saying the Lord's Prayer.

They were too inhibited, too self-distrustful, much too wrapped up in their own affairs; they said they were not "good" at Twelfth Stepping. How did they know? They never tried, as far as I could discern!

I'm sure that sometimes some experience of theirs must have matched that of the newcomer who was asking for help. But they remained silent and passed the buck to the others. Valuable help was lost many times, I'm sure.

Our responsibility in Al-Anon is to help others as we were helped. We have no professional Twelfth Steppers in Al-Anon—we wouldn't want them. But we do want the shared experience of all of us. Perhaps if there were a sign on each chair which said, "The Buck Stops Here," every member, no matter how shy, would share his experience.

Winnie-the-Pooh and Al-Anon

MANY OF US find ourselves in much the same fix as Milne's Pooh, who had promised to write a poem about Piglet's heroism and found the going difficult: "But it isn't easy," said Pooh to himself, "because Poetry and Hums aren't things which you get, they're things which get *you*. And all you can do is to go where they can find you."

So Pooh waited hopefully to see what happened, and a seven-verse poem happened, which he supposed had never been heard of before—not at least in the House at Pooh Corner.

In my very early days of Al-Anon, the First Step was very much on my mind. I thought of it constantly but found myself doing all the futile things I'd always done; I was as far from actually practicing that Step as if I'd never heard of it. Fortunately, I kept going to meetings—the place where it could find me—and eventually *it* did find *me* and I began living an Al-Anon life.

So it was with a dear friend. Dot had attended AA meetings with her husband for a long time. She was happy

Value of a Wastebasket

WE RECENTLY MOVED, after eight years in a fairly small apartment. It's lovely to have more room, marvelous to look out on the most spectacular view of the Hudson and the Palisades in the world—but accustomed things have an annoying way of not being where I instinctively reach for them.

Like my wastebasket: for eight years it has been beside my typewriter where I can drop paper in it without looking. The other day I sat down to work on the new FORUM. I put in a fresh sheet of paper and suddenly realized the wastebasket was not there—it was still in a glut of things unsorted and unplaced. And I froze up. I could not type a word until I had stopped, hunted it up and put it in its accustomed place. This bothered me for a time because I kept thinking, "Why can't you type without a wastebasket?"

When I had thought it out, I knew I was asking the wrong question. It should have been, "Why can't you write without a wastebasket?" And I knew I couldn't. I'm sure now it's best that I can't.

To begin with, there's nothing quite so cold as a fresh piece of white paper. Others may be inspired by such a challenge but I go sort of blank. No matter how much thought I have given my piece, how well I have planned its introduction, the first few lines on a new sheet of paper never quite express what I had planned. I drop down a bit and begin over, changing a word or two, or a phrase, until I've come as close as I believe I can to what I mean to say.

By the time I have a reasonable facsimile of what I want

to say, the wastebasket is deep in false starts, each one just a little bit closer to exactness.

For days now I've been thinking of writing and wastebaskets. I also wish everyone had a compulsive habit of a mental wastebasket when talking.

If, mentally, we could sort out the irrelevant, the obscure and the distracting things which keep us from expressing our exact meaning, conversation would be a thrilling and stimulating experience.

We'd have no difficulty in interpreting to newcomers just why they are powerless over alcohol, just how they make themselves "Let Go and Let God." There'd be no obscurity, no chance for misunderstanding.

It would be the millennium if we all talked as Churchill did. But we can try, at least. Here's for more and bigger mental wastebaskets.

"Enter to Learn; Go Forth to Teach"

SOMEONE recently queried the New York Times Book Section as to the source of the maxim, "Enter to learn; go forth to teach." I cannot identify the quotation but I can accept it as a perfect blueprint for good Al-Anon membership.

Most of us, but not all of course, enter Al-Anon to learn what magic button to press to turn an uncontrolled drinker into a model of sobriety.

We often do not even know that alcoholism is a disease. We just know our lives are a mess because of it and we want it stopped—right now, and for good. Why should we tolerate excess?

We know we are doing everything in our power to stop

the drinking, to outwit the imbiber and out maneuver him so that he can't get a drink.

Every unhappy thing in our lives is laid to drinking. None of it is our fault. Naturally! We don't drink to excess and therefore we are perfect. Or were *you* different?

That's where the beginning of wisdom occurs. First we learn there is no magic button. We learn alcoholism is a disease and the alcoholic has contracted it. We learn that all our "helpfulness" is an extra burden for the alcoholic to carry.

Occasionally we get a glimmer that our wings have molted a bit here and there and our halos have dulled over the years. Gradually we have come to recognize that we ourselves are less than perfect and can use the guides provided for us.

Thus, although we entered only to learn about the magic button, we did enter to learn. We did learn, too—not what we anticipated but what would really help us in our dilemma.

And having learned a great deal of what Al-Anon teaches—there's always something new so that we never graduate—we accept the obligation to "go forth to teach."

In our new-found gratitude for the help we have received, we wish to share our experience with those still suffering, still floundering as we floundered. By guiding others in the program, we strengthen our own practice of it.

By giving of ourselves, our beliefs, our practices, we are enriched beyond measure; our Al-Anon program becomes a stronger influence in our lives and our joy in it is increased a hundredfold.

We cannot selfishly hoard our joy and our helpfulness and still live our program. Thus I cannot think of a better maxim for us to follow than "Enter to learn; go forth to teach."

Tale of Two Frogs

MARY L.S., of San Diego, Cal., sent me a marvelously imaginative tale by which she has been living.

A farmhand carelessly left a freshly-milked pail of milk in the cowshed and went off to supper. Two frogs promptly jumped in.

One frog thrashed frantically around, exhausted himself and sank, discouraged, to the bottom. The other quietly moved his front and hind legs back and forth, easily keeping his head above the surface.

Next morning the farmhand returned to find the frog happily croaking, seated on a large blob of butter! When he dumped the now useless contents, the frog joyously went about his business. And down at the bottom was the first frog—dead.

As an old-time churner (I regularly churned during the ranch years), I heartily admire that second frog. Mary is grateful to him, too. She says that when she first heard the story it had little meaning for her. But since Al-Anon it reminds her always "neither to fight nor run away—just quietly to do the best I can with serenity, and I, too, may churn my blob of butter which will save my life and sanity."

Since Mary's letter came last November—it's taken all this time to find a place for it—I've been living with the second frog, too, deeply grateful to her for making us acquainted.

I have seldom, since Al-Anon, indulged in scenes or sought release from unpleasant circumstances by boiling over. Rather, I have created more tension within mself by mentally thrashing around until I have exhausted myself, when, fortunately, Al-Anon takes over and I again see things in perspective.

Mary's frog has happily shortened this period. I may not now have butter to show for my efforts but I do attain a better quality of serenity, more quickly.

Thoughts on Waste

WHEN MY DAUGHTER was away at college she wrote some humorous verses about her roommate which have always amused me. They ended, as I remember, "I now must add, before I stop, she *squeezes toothpaste from the top!*" These lines frequently come to mind when I hear people ask for more and more new Al-Anon literature.

Everyone knows that squeezing toothpaste from the top is wasteful and leads to difficulty as the paste is used. I used to do it, until I found I frequently was squeezing it messily through a break in the tube and it was virtually impossible to get all the paste out.

When I took the trouble to squeeze from the bottom—and I grant it is more trouble—it always came out neatly from the opening provided and I could use the entire contents of the tubes.

So, back to our Al-Anon literature; many times, when these requests for new pamphlets come, or when a group has got itself into difficulties and writes for help, a small amount of consideration shows that the situation has already been covered—the solution suggested. Either the writers have never read the literature, or they have simply skimmed it "from the top."

Spring is upon us—a good time to take a fresh look at our Al-Anon Conference Approved literature, so that the practice of our program may have new stimulus and growth, to make it match that of the burgeoning world about us.

A thoughtful review of our literature will not only repay you personally, in deepening your understanding of yourself and your family, it will enable you to be a better help to those still in need. It is too good to receive only the "once over lightly" treatment.

Adding a Cubit to Our Stature

DON'T YOU AGREE there's a tie between not practicing the First Step and holding resentments? Perhaps one leads inevitably to the other but both stand on their own feet as menaces to good practice of Al-Anon.

We are told that "No man, by taking thought, can add a cubit to his stature." Since a cubit varies from 17+ to 20+ inches, I can't see who would like to add one physically. But I do believe most of us would like to add several spiritually. And it is exactly by taking thought that we can do so.

Today let's think of resentments. To me, harboring resentments is a lot like encasing ourselves in a surrounding shell like the bullet-proof shield they show on TV where nothing, not even high-powered ammunition, penetrates. Nothing enters; nothing goes forth—everything bounces off.

Holding resentments is much like that. Nothing changes; our reaction is always the same to a given situation. And as long as we foster and feed the resentment by a customary reaction, just so long do we remain static, or grow worse.

If we resent slips—and I don't expect anyone to welcome them—and react by raising Cain ourselves, we don't progress.

If we work on the acceptance of alcoholism as a disease and train ourselves to accept a slip as a symptom of that disease, we are on the way to overcoming resentment of the slip.

We are freeing ourselves from a bit of the prison we have erected about ourselves. Some little help has a chance to penetrate our shield, even though it is only the thought that "This, too, shall pass." If we recognize that the situation will not last forever, we can better cope with it.

Thus, by giving thought, instead of reacting in an established, unhelpful way, we can increase our tolerance, reduce our resentment.

Few of us, if any, can change overnight. We are not snakes who shed outworn skins in a moment and instantly emerge in shining new ones.

We may have to set stakes to measure our forward progress. But by giving sufficient thought to what Al-Anon teaches us, we can gradually add to our spiritual stature, one infinitesimal bit at a time, until those bits add up to a cubit.

Which Is in Control—You or Panic?

"FEAR IS THE BEGINNING of all weakness." I don't remember where I picked that up but the more thought it is given, the truer it is that fear is the beginning of most, if not of all, weaknesses.

Robert Frost expressed the same thought in a slightly different way: "The people I am most scared of are the people who are scared."

If your mind is in a welter of fear, no matter of what, you cannot possibly do a job of clear thinking and arrive at a good solution. I am not speaking of the kind of fear of accident which makes us wait for green lights at street crossings instead of darting out in the middle of traffic. That is only common sense.

I do mean the kind of fear which envelops us when we forget that today is all the time we have, when we get ourselves into a quivering mess of fear of tomorrow or next year or ten years from now.

That kind of fear can do nothing but harm. All it can do is weaken us, prevent us from making our best effort to plan sanely and wisely for whatever comes. The worst thing about such a fear is that each time we allow ourselves to become a prey to it, it makes it easier to succumb a second time, and a third, until we become afraid of everything.

The solution is not easy. But there is a solution.

Should you find yourself faced with a situation which normally would throw you into a nervous collapse of uncontrolled fear, quietly sit down and try to put everything out of your mind for a bit. Then face your fear: analyze it; pursue it until you determine what really is the absolute worst that could happen.

Perhaps this will be too difficult for you to do alone. If so, by all means talk it over with someone in whom you have confidence, someone who has had a like experience and is competent to help—not just a hand-holder, a shoulder-patter, and a listening post.

Then, having pursued your fear to its bitter end, and having recognized it for the craven thing it probably is, there is no further place to go but onwards.

Courage will replace the nameless fears which are so frightening. Calmness will come to enable you to face whatever comes. You—not panic—will be in control.

Peace Within Ourselves

MARGARET MEAD once said that we are the first generation in history which is asked to ponder the entire world's ills with our morning coffee. Communication is so instant today that every disaster comes upon us with the shock of current happening.

When men went to the Crusades, or when clipper ships sailed to the Orient, news of disasters was brought home years later with the cushion of time behind it, and thus was easier to bear.

In spite of this, we do not want to shut ourselves away from the world—most of us would, indeed, find it impossible to do so. Our salvation lies in getting things into proper perspective, so that when the world's woes hit us at the same time we are under personal strain, we can keep from going under by concentrating on what is possible for us to do to ease the strain. The three parts of the Serenity Prayer are our best help here.

"Every crime is punished," wrote Emerson; "the swindler only swindles himself . . . there's no penalty for virtue, wisdom, love, beauty. When these are considered in their purest sense, they bring the sweetest of rewards—peace within ourselves."

If we keep swindling ourselves by eternally struggling against the things we cannot change, we are the worst losers. It is a sad consequence that those about us lose also, because we are not creating a tranquil home.

But if we can lift ourselves above these crippling distractions, these unhappy distortions, we can free our minds and renew our spirits to improve everything around us.

If we successfully suppress impotent rebellion and concentrate only upon achieving a quiet calm, we'll have that greatest gift of all, "peace within ourselves." Everyone about us will share in our serenity.

Twelfth Step Warm-Up

HAVE YOU EVER seemed to fail on a Twelfth Step call, retired within yourself and decided you were just no good at it? If so, do remember this: good Twelfth Step work isn't always accomplished easily. Except for a fortunate few, most of us have to practice, and practice!

It has been proved, also, that seeming failure seldom is actual failure. Sometimes the person you call on isn't ready for help.Or perhaps he doesn't identify with you. (Even the best talks we hear in group meetings understandably fail to identify with every listener.)

But the few words you say of what Al-Anon has done for you may kindle a tiny spark to light the darkness. Buried deep, perhaps even out of mind, they may remain in the subconscious until the need is imperative.

That spark then bursts into flame and the person is ready for the hope and help Al-Anon can so generously give, through you or some other Al-Anon member.

Uninformed people living with the problem of alcoholism, trying to cope with it all alone, not unnaturally are frequently touchy. Personally, even with sponsors as experienced as Lois and Dot, I was a prickly pear for months, shutting them off as frequently as I could. But they refused to entertain hurt feelings—kept the contact and waited until I was ready to open my eyes and my mind.

It is better, I believe, to offer help too soon than to risk being too late. Our shoulders broaden in Al-Anon: we can accept rebuffs and not be crippled by resentments. We don't want just to stand by like the two hesitant ladies who sat by the lakeshore, watching a drowning man come up for the third time and said, "Oh dear, oh dear, why DOESN'T he cry for help!"

Should your helpful offer be unwelcome, you easily can withdraw. Later, if the person comes to you and asks to learn more of the program, you then can speak freely.

If assistance is asked of someone else, that is fine and not an occasion for hurt feelings or a conclusion that you are not good at Twelfth Stepping. Perhaps it's because you needed a little more practice. Perhaps you pushed too hard, too soon, in your enthusiasm, and he wasn't quite ready.

If a response is negative, console yourself with the thought that you have lit a spark and didn't let someone sink before he cried for help.

Bounty of Al-Anon

ONE REWARD for the consistent observance of the Al-Anon program is the unexpected light it frequently sheds upon ideas and problems apart from the program itself.

Like the time I wrote about before when I fumed because a car down the street blocked the sidewalk and I thought I'd have to go into the road to pass it. Just as I approached it, with ten extra pounds of blood pressure from exasperation, the car drove off; my way was clear. I was disturbed when "Easy Does It" and "The 24 Hour Program" popped into my mind: I'd got all worked up over something which never happened.

A more startling coincidence occurred just the other day which cast light on an idea I'd cherished a very long time.

A thousand years ago, more or less, when I was in school, a professor told of Margaret Fuller's proclamation, "I accept the Universe!" He went on to repeat Carlyle's comment, when he heard of her announcement: "She damn well better!"

Although I knew Margaret Fuller was considered a brilliant woman, a Transcendentalist, one of the earliest champions of equal rights for women and among the foremost critics of her time, I immediately put her down as a silly show-off. Carlyle's comment seemed well merited, if abrupt. All these years I've had a smug sense of superiority whenever I've thought of her.

Last week, something brought her to mind. As usual, my first thought was, "Silly show-off. What else could she do?" I was not thinking of Al-Anon, at least not consciously. But instantly, and for the first time, it flashed upon me that she had actually gained the wisdom I pray for "to accept the things I cannot change."

My long-established smugness was shattered. Suddenly bereft of an idea which had long been part of me, I felt a deep sense of chagrin that I had so greatly misjudged another person. I was indeed grateful it couldn't matter to Margaret Fuller—dead more than a hundred years—what I had thought of her. But it did give me pause when I wondered what other misconceptions I still might cherish, ones which could matter.

The bounty of Al-Anon, to me, is the power it gives us to change thoughts and habits of a lifetime, to shed old prejudices, and to gain new insights into murky places.

Mark Twain's Cat

We should be careful to get out of an experience only the wisdom that is in it, and stop there, lest we be like the cat that sits down on a hot stove-lid. She will never sit down on a hot stove-lid again—and that is well, but also she will never sit on a cold one anymore.

Mark Twain

How many times have you tried something, failed dismally, and said, "Never again! That's not for me." Perhaps it isn't and perhaps it is—it may be a cold stove-lid which just looked hot. Too often, I believe, we shut ourselves away from accomplishment by giving up too readily.

If you are inhibited, shy and easily embarrassed, you probably find it difficult to speak at open meetings; if you are a perfectionist, very likely you have little patience with yourself at being less than a golden-tongued orator.

Thus you may prefer to make your contribution to the group and the program by helping with chores. This is all very well; the jobs have to be done and you contribute to the smooth running of the group by doing them.

But should you stop there? Making coffee never explained our program to anyone. Your experience in Al-Anon, or the particular thing which most helped you, perhaps may be just the thing which would bring the whole program into focus for someone else.

At first, telling your story might be like sitting on a hot lid. But as you discipline yourself to speak in public, you most likely will find that the lid becomes cooler and cooler.

A once-over-lightly approach to our program accomplishes nothing. You have to persist in practicing the difficult parts, as well as the easy ones. Persistence, not quitting, pays off.

If you tackle those things which are most difficult for you, one at a time, instead of plunging wholesale into general reform, you'll have a greater chance of success.

You can learn to distinguish which lids stay hot and which cool off.

The Best Years of Our Lives

IT'S SADDENING to think so many people are afraid of age. Today's emphasis in the U.S. and seemingly in England with Twiggy, the Beatles, Mods and all that genre, is on youth—not "flaming youth" as between wars but just youth.

Such great importance given to lack of years makes many regret theirs have increased. Lately I heard a man of 50-odd say, seriously, that by then "the best years" are gone.

This seems nonsense to me. Worse, I feel it is idiotic. I don't believe I feel so strongly about this because I have "silver threads among the gold." I no longer do. They've changed from silver to ivory. But even when they all shone pure gold I felt the same.

Probably I owe this feeling to the most brilliant man I ever knew—a diagnostician and researcher, in his mid-forties. I was his secretary, in my mid-twenties.

One day I found him reading a magazine I considered trifling. He'd come early to read it before it was put in the reception room and carelessly carried off.

Horrified, I said, "WHAT are YOU doing with that trash? I don't read it and I haven't a tenth your brain!" He smiled and said, "My dear, I'm 45. I consider that by now I cannot harm my brain. I feel I can do with it as I like."

That thought gave me pause for days. I decided I would never be afraid of any birthday—30, 40, even 70 or 80. Each would find me ready, perhaps would free me of some restriction but surely would give me a better perspective of what was important and what nonessential. Happily, that is exactly how it is working out.

How can we put our best effort into what we do if part of our mind is concentrated on regretting lost youth, or if part is off with the gypsies speculating on a future of more years? This why our 24-hour program is so logical and so valuable.

No one of us knows how much time we'll have. But even if the present moment is bad, our program shows us how to live through it without giving up. We have gained resources to help us.

If we live each day completely, to the best of our ability, according to our program, not looking back in regret nor forward in despair, we are sure to attain maturity. And no really mature person, I believe, can agree that the best years of our lives are over until there are no more years.

Christmas and Al-Anon

EVER THINK how much Christmas and Al-Anon have in common? Both are based on love; both bring joy and hope to the world, lift our spirits and fill our hearts with kindness toward all.

Christmas climaxes a year in which we may or may not have done all we could for our fellow-man. It frequently inspires us to think of new ways we can give of ourselves. It gives us impetus toward doing more for others.

Christmas is not only a day—it is a time and it is a feeling. This time and this feeling are where it is most like Al-Anon. Our fellowship has restored us to mental and spiritual health, returned joy to our lives and made us keenly aware that we need keep practicing Al-Anon principles daily, in all our affairs.

We cannot let our program be a one-day anniversary, no matter how great and good the occasion we celebrate. We need to "get it and give it," every day in some way. We cannot hoard it to ourselves, or it will wither away. The more we give of the program to another, the more meaningful it is to us and the stronger we become in rooting out weakness in ourselves.

Thus it seems to me that Al-Anon is a year round Christmas—we get help and we give it. We are happy and we show others how to attain happiness. We are blessed and we share our blessings.

May every Christmas joy be yours and may Al-Anon strengthen and guide you all through the year.

Where Does Twelfth Step Work End?

. . . it begins with you but did you ever wonder just how far it stretches?

You know the joy and the thrill of seeing hope rekindle when, after a talk at an open meeting, people come to say you have cast light in a dark place. But does the help stop there?

The longer I am in Al-Anon and the more letters to the FORUM I read, the more I realize that helping someone never stops with the first person helped.

I am an utter moron at Physics and cannot understand

that a ripple, caused by a stone cast into water, goes on and on, into infinity.

Even were the stone cast into the sea, I'd think the ripple soon would peter out; if cast into a pond, surely it must stop at the shore? But it doesn't take Physics to make me see the widespread effect of Al-Anon Twelfth Stepping.

At my first meeting, a stranger changed my life by her talk; I've never told of that meeting without having four to a dozen people—AAs as well as Al-Anons—tell me I'd taken an intolerable burden from them. How many more have been helped by these dozens (and the dozens reached by those dozens) it's impossible to guess. Her story and its effect on me must, by now, have reached hundreds and thousands, I'm sure.

When she made that talk, I'm equally sure she had no idea of affecting anyone beyond the eight or ten members there.

One cannot know what effect something will have. I remember telling in Cleveland of the countless things I did to keep my husband from the first drink.

I had planned my talk carefully, had typed it out several times to boil it down and gone over it countless times so that I could speak easily.

But as I recounted my endless, futile attempts, quite spontaneously I added, "The only thing I didn't do was the one thing I should have done—NOTHING."

Years later, at Toronto, someone spoke of the great help she'd had from my Cleveland talk: "What you said about doing nothing has kept me from trying to run things ever since! I'll never forget it and never stop practicing it."

Someone quoted in a letter to the FORUM, years ago, "Fear knocked at the door. Faith answered and lo!, there was no one there." It was printed as a Stopper. Many times since, I've heard it quoted at meetings.

Also I know of a young woman who has lived by it for the eight years since she read it in the FORUM. Furthermore she is teaching her three children to live by it, too.

God bless the person who sent it in. She can't know how much good she did for so many but the good still carries on.

Perhaps Shakespeare said it all, more concisely, in "How far that little candle throws his beams!" But eventually the little beam can no longer be seen. Al-Anon Twelfth Step influence, however, goes on and on, gaining strength as it reaches each new person. May its impetus never lessen until there no longer is need anywhere in this whole world.

Getting Fit to Live

A BOOK which Bill, co-founder of AA, frequently refers to as an influence in his life and in the formation of AA, is William James's *The Varieties of Religious Experience*.

Because of my great love and admiration for Bill, my endless gratitude for his part in the miracle of AA, I recently read it. It more than repaid me.

James's answer to part of a questionnaire he filled out in 1904 particularly impressed me:

"Q. Do you believe in personal immortality? Ans. Never keenly but more strongly as I grow older.

"Q. If so, why? Ans. Because I am just getting fit to live."

James at that time was 62!

Whether or not one believes in personal immortality is not important here. But "Because I am just getting fit to live" should be graven, I believe, on the hearts of every Al-Anon member.

Perhaps you were different—not as I was—pre-Al-Anon. On looking back now, from considerable experience in our fellowship, I can readily see that I was not really fit to live before it. I was withdrawn, resentful, incapable of a healthy, outgoing life. My own problems and unhappiness occupied me fully. It was not a life.

Every group to which I have belonged, every Al-Anon I've really talked with, has taught me things I needed to know or to remember in order to be fit to live.

Every letter I have received in my work on the FORUM has added its share; I have been favored beyond my deserts—I gratefully acknowledge it.

But each of us does have the program to follow; if truly lived and honestly followed, it can make all of us fit to live.

If it worked for the mess I was, it can work for you.

It did work for me, thank God. But in case you think I'm measuring myself for a halo, I'm not. By working for me, I mean the old bitterness is gone; the self-preoccupation is shattered; my horizons are widened to include the world. If that is not succeeding, if it is not becoming fit to live, remember, I am still in Al-Anon, still working at the program and it will carry me farther, as long as I stay with it.

The more you put into it, by study of the literature, by going to meetings, and by extending a generous helping hand to anyone in difficulty with some part of the program, the more fit you'll make yourself to live.

Putting Away Childish Things

REMEMBER WHEN we did "number work" back in the early grades? The multiplication tables and the "gazintas"? Perhaps you carefully said "two goes into six three times" but in our young words we rattled it off so that it came out gazintas.

All that was fine for that age. But Einstein could never have figured his complicated equations on number work, though he undoubtedly began his schooling with it. It took advanced study and years of higher mathematics as a foundation for his later work.

Entering Al-Anon is like our number work! It's a beginning we all must make in order to go on to other things. At first, just learning that we are not alone in our problem is enough.

Then we are told alcoholism is a disease for which we are not responsible. With this, the burden of failure begins to be lifted from us and resentment of the alcoholic begins to drop away. Who, in his right mind, can hold anyone responsible for a disease he had contracted?

With these three basics (knowledge we are no longer alone, have not failed in our jobs as mates, and alcoholism is a disease) we glimpse, and are anxious to return to, a normal life. They are Al-Anon's first gift.

Perhaps just these three facts are enough to enable some people to keep on an even keel for years and for their lives to be like the old fairy tales, happy ever after. Perhaps—just perhaps.

To my mind, old habits of thought, old patterns of behavior, are so strongly ingrained that I believe these three facts constitute only a firm foundation for a new approach to life.

It takes valiant, continuous work to overcome entrenched ideas, especially where we have always thought ourselves right and others wrong.

Resentments and self-pity are not always killed with a single blow—not even usually. We frequently believe they are. But we learn to our horror they more likely are akin to the Hydra who, when one head was cut off, grew two in its place.

Sometimes people tire of Al-Anon. They think they have learned all it can teach. They believe they have "graduated" from it and prefer to do something else each week, rather than go to a meeting. So they stop going.

Without the stimulation of the group, and without the impetus toward Al-Anon thinking provided at meetings, most of them soon find themselves slipping into old ways of thought. The fortunate ones return before much damage is done.

There is so much depth to the Al-Anon program, so many ways to interpret its teachings, that it is difficult for me to see how any one person could ever think he knew it all.

The odds I sometimes see on the chances of holding certain combinations of cards in bridge hands always make me dizzy. So it is when I think of the number of different applications people have made of the same Al-Anon principle. They are endless—and endlessly helpful.

I am happy I learned the three basic facts in Al-Anon. But, just as Einstein needed more than "number work" for his equations, so do I need more and deeper study for my adult life in Al-Anon. I hope I have "put away childish things" and never stop learning, by continued advanced study, the infinite riches of the Al-Anon philosophy.

Thoughts on Stretching the Mind

OLIVER WENDELL HOLMES's memory had a special place in my youth. My father was a member of the last class he taught at Harvard Medical School. As a memento, he copied out a whole stanza from "The Boys" on the flyleaf of his Collected Poems, autographed it and gave it to my father.

Perhaps that fact, plus my long ago, superficial reading of him, contributed to my great surprise when I came upon a quotation from him recently: "Stretch the mind and it never goes back." That didn't fit anything I ever associated with Holmes but it did bring me up short.

"Stretch the mind." What other aim should life have? I don't want to seem pedantic nor be overly "Stern-Daughter-of-the-voice-of God"-ish, but I do believe all our experiences should contribute to a wider, deeper understanding of life and a better ability to adjust ourselves to it.

That is why our program is so precious and helpful to me. Before Al-Anon, I was in constant rebellion against the turmoil in my life because of my inability to accept and adjust to difficulties connected with alcoholism.

I was over-fond of dismissing the whole thing as, "This is too dusty a life—I was meant for better things."

Strangely enough, I was exactly right; I WAS meant to have a better life. Every one of us is. But that better life has to be earned.

It took Al-Anon to show me how to live this better life. Instead of constantly rolling around the idea of what was due me, Al-Anon opened my eyes to the surprising fact that *I had made my life what it was.* My own rebellion, my resentments, had blinded and sickened me.

Al-Anon—and it didn't come easily nor quickly—showed me that my life could be what I made it. By truly accepting my powerlessness over alcohol, by realizing that I, myself, had allowed my life to become unmanageable, I was able to ask and receive help in restoring myself to sanity with help from my Higher Power and help from my fellow-members.

The first time I really understood that I was my own worst enemy, that I was making my own difficulties, my mind began to stretch. It did not stretch all the way for quite a long time. I slipped back at times to self-pity and rebellion. But I did keep trying. The stretch reached just a little bit farther each time.

Now, with a perspective of long years between me and that old rebellious self, I can see I am a better person than before; it took all those upsets and heartbreaks to jolt me out of my complacency. Had I never had difficulties to surmount, I'd still be thinking of what was due me, not of what I should be doing to justify my being.

Life is a gift and an obligation. Unless we develop beyond the infant stage where we are wholly dependent upon what is done for us, without any thought of repayment, we are simply takers. We are living only a part of the life we were meant to live.

I was not happy through many of the drinking years. I can now see, however, that it took them to teach me my need of the Al-Anon program and my responsibility to those who need it now.

Al-Anon stretched my mind and it never can go back.

"Look for a Long Time"

LATELY I've been sad though I knew it was a "thing I cannot change." A line quoted by Robert Phelps in his preface to Colette's autobiography, Earthly Paradise, set me straight.

Colette, he says, once advised a young writer: "Look for a long time at what pleases you, and longer still at what pains you."

That bothered me considerably at first; it seemed totally against Al-Anon. Why couldn't I accept what had happened? But I couldn't.

My older brother was ill in Chicago with no hope of recovery but he could have lived months. Two urgent things kept me in New York: I had to finish March's FORUM and attend our quarterly Trustees' Board meeting. Then I took the first plane out.

I arrived to learn my brother had died in the night. Grateful as I was he hadn't suffered, thankful he'd known I was coming, I couldn't adjust myself to missing him by so little.

Death is always a shock, even when preceded by illness. All the past, a shared childhood, the growing up years and mutual joys and sorrows—those can't help but crowd one's mind and dim the sun when the one you spent them with is gone. I have adjusted to them in the past but what I could not endure was such a near miss.

When I read, "Look longer still at what pains you," I put the book down and went over everything in my mind in an inventory different from our Fourth Step but just as searching.

I found I was simply sorry for myself. Could I have said or done anything not already said or done for Jim? I saw I wasn't mourning for him but was sad because I'd missed him by so few hours. My grief was self-pity, reluctance to let go.

When I finally understood I was pitying myself, that it was me I was sorry for, I began to feel better. After all, those years and those joys are still in my mind. They live with me.

When I looked long enough I realized that missing Jim by half a day or half a year was not important. He is at rest and at peace, I am sure. He's had a good, useful life for the most part. Had he lived something might have developed which entailed suffering. Why should I ask more?

If you're sad, "Look long at what pleases you, and longer still at what pains you." It helps.

A "Tranquilizer" Highly Recommended

IN MARCH I spent a most rewarding weekend in Monroe, Louisiana, at the AA Birthday Party. Al-Anon had a place on the program and I flew down to speak. As always I had a wonderful time—Al-Anons and AAs are the most cordial, generous and appreciative audience one can find anywhere. They are more enthusiastic than children at a circus.

My flight home was via New Orleans, which I had never visited. At the last moment I changed my ticket so I could spend a day there, seeing a bit of that most interesting city.

Out at Lake Pontchartrain I learned hurricane warnings were up, which did little to make me anticipate my flight the next day. I've lived through two already and can't recommend them as good entertainment.

Next noon we took off in fairly decent weather which soon deteriorated until nothing could be seen from my window but the heaviest fog I've ever flown through.

About the time we were due to land at Kennedy airport, the stewardess announced we were coming in for a landing. I waited for hours for the NO SMOKING sign to come on.

Nothing happened.

Reports I'd read recently about planes hijacked and flown to Cuba inevitably came to mind. They'd included the detail that no announcement of a change in destination had been permitted, so that as time went on I became surer and surer we were headed for Havana and trouble.

If the fog was disturbing, that thought was worse. I had wondered before how long the Cubans were going to allow planes to land and take off without penalty; now my fervent hope was they hadn't changed their policy.

I'm not the worrywart I used to be but I cannot say I was wholly at my best. Then Al-Anon rescued me.

"Can I stop this fog? Can I do one single thing about where we're going to put down? We are seven miles up above the earth—what can I do about it?" Answers were unanimously negative. Wasn't this, then, "a thing I couldn't change?"

"Where is your Al-Anon?" I asked myself. "You travel thousands of miles to tell your experience in Al-Anon, hoping to help someone else. How can you possibly expect to be anything but a tinkling cymbal or sounding brass if YOU don't practice the program yourself. Better pull up your socks and get at it."

It took no wisdom to know I was in a situation I couldn't change, so no courage was involved in needlessly trying to change it. The only thing left was to seek serenity to accept whatever eventuated. I just concentrated on that: "I am in God's hands. His will, not mine, be done. Live as you'd like to die, in trust and hope, and not in craven fear."

So I stopped gluing my eyes to my watch and went back to reading my paperback murder. An hour or so later the stewardess announced that we were above Kennedy and would "hold" for forty-five minutes while other planes landed ahead of us.

Little as I like "holding" at any time, in a blinding fog I hate it. But by then I had enough serenity to realize immediately I was powerless in this situation too. Again I returned to my mystery and read another hour until we put down in a cloudburst. I thanked God and gratefully got off.

Next morning my *Times* carried an account of another plane which was hijacked to Cuba the day before!

Later I had a lovely note from Monroe, thanking me for my talk, in which Theresa told me someone had said at their meeting, "If Margaret had flown today, she might have been on that plane—think of it!"

"I said," wrote Theresa, "if she had been, she'd probably just do a piece in the FORUM about it." How right she was and how well she knew me! I was in the midst of writing this very article when her note came and I hadn't even been hijacked. I laugh every time I think of it.

But what it all amounts to is that for someone who had such initial and prolonged difficulty in getting our program, I have to concentrate on it constantly and keep on "practicing it in ALL my affairs."

Should any of you find yourself seven miles above the earth, in a blinding fog, I cannot recommend too highly asking to be granted "the serenity to accept the things you cannot change" and to "Let Go and Let God."

Don't Let It Throw You

NOTHING I HAVE ever heard or read indicated that life was meant to be one sweet song after another. No one promised there'd never be a discordant note nor a major disappointment.

But all too often such happenings occur. When they do, many of us catch ourselves thinking that life is more difficult today then ever before. Is it?

Job had enough set-backs for a regiment. His unshaken

belief, "Blessed is the man whom God correcteth" was enough to keep him going. He lived through all afflictions and was rewarded greatly.

When General Anthony C. McAuliffe, trapped for a week at Bastogne in the Battle of the Bulge, was presented with an ultimatum from the Germans, demanding he surrender the remnants of his 101st Airborne Division, he kept up his courage, and that of all his men, with his offhand and contemptuous "Nuts."

These are extreme examples of life's hazards. Few of us are likely to find ourselves in such desperate circumstances. But are we meeting much lesser ills with like acceptance? How often do we quail before really minor difficulties?

We set ourselves a goal, even work diligently toward reaching it. When we fail, fall short of accomplishing all of it, all too often we say, "I can't do that. It's too hard for me."

Maybe we did fail at first. But that shouldn't throw us. Perhaps our aim was set too high for the time being. Rather than abandon that goal, it would be better for us to put it aside for a while and attack it a bit later, when we are more prepared, have more knowledge.

All of us have seen newcomers come to Al-Anon, filled with enthusiasm for the program. They eagerly accept what they are told, and are overjoyed if their partners go into AA. But let misfortune come and that partner unhappily has a slip, they abandon everything and say to themselves, "Why should I continue in Al-Anon if George is going to drink?" So they leave the group.

It does little good to remind these people that we work at this program to get help for ourselves, not to sober up our spouses. They have been completely thrown by the first adversity.

If they would refuse to be thus thrown, if they'd pick

themselves up after just a little stumble, attack the program anew, listen with more open minds and apply what they hear, most likely they'd achieve success. At least their own lives would be more tranquil.

Queerly enough, by reaching that enviable state, their partners often are inspired to reach it too. Success almost inevitably crowns the efforts of those who refuse to be thrown.

Giving up is easy enough. But it almost always leads to more trouble. When disaster comes, or even just minor disappointment, say to yourself, "Don't let it throw me." Give yourself a rest and begin over again.

Through Other Eyes

PROUST HAS ALWAYS seemed beyond my powers of concentration so that I've never really disciplined myself to take on his "Remembrance of Things Past." But a quotation I came upon recently delighted me.

It said, in effect, it would do us little good to grow wings and to develop different breathing so that we could voyage into space, if our own senses remained unchanged.

According to Proust a voyage of discovery would be possible only if we looked through "other eyes, to behold the universe through the eyes of another, of a hundred others, to behold the hundred universes that each of them beholds, that each of them is."

This enchanted me. It instantly brought back a summer day, several years ago, when I sat and watched one of my favorite grandsons (I have two!) make a candy house which absorbed and delighted him.

He had cut the ends of a small carton into triangles to

form peaks and had fitted cardboard over them to make a roof. He'd glued graham crackers, smeared sketchily with a white frosting, to cover the house's sides and was busy dipping gum-drops into egg white to make them stick to the roof.

He frowned when he saw that only a few gum-drops were left, while half the roof was still bare. "Honey," I said, "those gum-drops are flat, top and bottom. I think if you'd make three slices of them, they would cover the roof."

Happily the idea worked, even though the effect of bumpy, whole gum-drops and flat slices of them was on the bizarre side. To his six-year-old eyes, it was obviously beautiful.

My daughter joined us for a moment and afterwards said, "Mommie, you were completely absorbed by Billy's house. What were you thinking about?" "I was just thinking that I'd give a million to be able to see that house through Billy's eyes," I answered—and then forgot it.

My daughter is an elephant for memory; she really listens and never forgets. Months later she reminded me of it; told me she hadn't been able to get it out of her mind. Every time she became impatient, trying to understand something silly Billy had done, she had remembered my wish to see his house through his eyes, and had relaxed.

Those few words of Proust brought all this back—made me realize that if we judge and value everything about us only by our own experience and standards, we don't really grow or develop.

But if we bother "to look through the eyes of another," a whole new world can reveal itself to us, even in our everyday surroundings. Fifteen minutes of such looking could do more for us, I believe, mentally and spiritually, than any other exercise.

Try looking through the eyes of another and see what you discover.

"When You Can't Do as You Would . . ."

THE LAST PLACE in the world one would expect to come upon Al-Anon philosophy is in a gardening book, published almost a hundred years ago. But there it was, waiting for me to find it.

I read it because I admired the spunky author, not because of need for the gardening lore in it. We live in an aerie overlooking the Hudson, a sixteenth floor apartment with not even a windowbox. The only plants we have are lilies at Easter, poinsettias at Christmas and a pot of chives which die every time we go away.

"Gardening by Myself" was written by Anna B. Warner in 1872 when she was past fifty. She and her sister lived alone on Constitution Island, opposite West Point, in very straitened circumstances after having enjoyed great wealth. She wrote twenty books and collaborated with her sister Susan on nineteen more, many of them best-sellers in their day.

An avid gardener, Anna's great love was a profusion of flowers. Winter nights she pored over catalogues and planned how best to spend the little money she could spare for seeds.

She never regretted her inability to afford the expensive new offerings, although she read every glowing word about them. She simply looked forward to the day when she could buy them. As she wrote, "What I can afford must come even before what I want," and the price of one seed of an untried novelty would buy packets of five to ten reliable old favorites. I was glad to read that she did occasionally plunge, on a less expensive new seed.

She wrote that gardeners frowned upon planting seeds in pots instead of in professional flats. She did not have flats and could neither afford them nor build them herself. Thus she made do—quite successfully, too—with pots. "When you can't do as you would," she wrote, "you must do as you can."

After Susan's death when Anna was sixty-five, she lived quite alone on the island for thirty years until her death in 1915. If anyone commented upon her solitary life she always said, "I am not alone; God is with me."

On almost every page of her little book there is some reflection of the acceptance and serenity we strive for in Al-Anon. She never looked back in regret and she never looked forward with anxiety.

I think of her many times when I hear someone at a meeting castigating herself for something done in the past. One woman I know cannot forgive herself for hospitalizing her husband, because he resented it so greatly. I feel it was all she could do at the time: he had the entire family in such fear and uproar they had to be protected temporarily. I agree with Miss Anna, "When you can't do as you would, you must do as you can."

Few, if any, of us live lives of such perfect acceptance as Miss Anna did. She had no need of Al-Anon; apparently she was born with the whole program at her fingertips.

We are different. We do need it. And, through Al-Anon, we can follow in her footsteps, daily to come nearer our goal of serenity.

What Do You Want?

"THE MOST frightening people are those who do not know what they want; we therefore must devote all our energy to the business of making our wishes completely clear." **Maxim Gorky.**

Anyone who has lived through a hurricane remembers it for an experience he would not like repeated. Yet, pre-Al-Anon, many of us were violently blown about by storms at home, yet always went back for repeat performances.

Many wished we had never met our partners and thus would have escaped present circumstances. Or many wished we had recognized the situation before children arrived. And many more wished for an end, any end, to the mess in which we lived. Only a blind sense of responsibility or habit had made us remain with an alcoholic partner.

The truth is that we really didn't know what we wanted, that we were frightened, vacillating people. In our confusion we simply felt that if the drinking partner stopped drinking, everything would be all right.

Then came the Al-Anon program to set us straight, to give us goals and purpose. It taught us that what happens to a person is not nearly so important as what we do about the happening, how we meet whatever comes with it.

When the Al-Anon program showed us a goal of serenity and acceptance amid whatever confusion existed, we stopped being helplessly tossed about. We stopped our childish rebellion which expressed itself in transitory dreams of escape. We stopped being potential time-bombs, ready to explode upon any provocation.

When Al-Anon centered our desires upon an ordered, meaningful life, and showed us how to attain it, we at last began to mature, to become useful, valuable as human beings, instead of frightened, frightening, haunted spirits.

Deciding what we want to be, and bending every effort toward making ourselves as near to that person as possible, is our main purpose in Al-Anon. It can, and in fact has, changed the lives of thousands.

One Day's FORUM Mail

IF IT WERE possible to reward each good letter, item or idea sent to the FORUM, I believe the best award possible would be to have the contributor of it sit at my desk for a day.

You all know by now the joy I have in editing the FORUM. Many of you have heard me say I wouldn't change places even with Lois, who really got Al-Anon going, when she and Anne first began work on a few names given them by the AA General Office. Bless them both, because I edit the FORUM as a result of their work.

Never-ending, always fascinating, dovetailing of experience, inspiration, joy in success, courage in adverse circumstances, generosity of spirit—all these are shared in letters to the FORUM. Reading them and putting them together is like working out a jig-saw puzzle.

This piece goes here; it came from South Dakota. That piece which came from New Zealand, goes next it, and a third from France, perhaps, fits above both. A whole friendly world spreads itself before me.

Take Adele's letter from Las Vegas, Nevada, in this FORUM. She, with Al-Anon's help, had learned acceptance, had realized that a compelling drive for impossible perfection could ruin her life.

At the same time, Teresa R., our WSD from Tennessee, sent in a wonderful bit she'd heard at an AA meeting; the speaker said he "had attained peace of mind somewhere between his ambitions and his limitations."

If those two letters do not belong together, neither do bread and butter. And they are of prime importance to all of us. They have a large part of our program wrapped up in them.

Too many of us set ourselves impossible goals. We perhaps try to do too much too soon. If we accomplish even half what we aim at, we may well be doing more than could really be expected of us. But because we did not attain everything we wanted, we feel we failed.

No one likes to live with failure, so we become discouraged. We may go so far wrong through discouragement, as to stop trying. Right here Adele's acceptance, and Teresa's AA speaker, have our answer: absolute perfection is beyond any of us. Peace of mind comes from a realistic appraisal of our ambitions, goals, limitations and accomplishments.

Each of us has his own job to do in life. Someone else might be able to do it better. But he is probably having a struggle to do his own job the best way he can.

I probably can do my grandson's spelling lessons to the Queen's taste, in no time flat and with no effort. But I'm an adult who has spent a lifetime learning, and he's a little boy, just at the beginning. I sometimes have problems in my own life and work, which are just as difficult for me.

The main point, as I see it, is to begin SOMEWHERE and KEEP AT IT. We have much to help us in our program. "Just For Today," "Take It Easy," the Serenity Prayer, and above all, innumerable accounts at meetings which testify to what Al-Anon has done to make countless lives happy again. All these are ours, just for the effort of listening, and practicing them.

Our main goal is serenity and peace of mind. If others have succeeded in reaching them, we can, too. And if I never can reward those writers of the most helpful messages, I need not upset myself. I can always print the letters!

Merry Christmas to Al-Anons and Alateens

MY DEARS:

Again my wish for you this year is like last year's: "May every Christmas joy be yours and may Al-Anon strengthen and guide you all through the year."

Twelve months have passed since that was written. In the same article I said that Christmas is not only a day but a time and feeling, that we cannot let our program be a one-day anniversary, that we need to "get it and give it" every day in some way. It's a good habit to establish.

Now, near the end of this old year and the beginning of a new one, it seems appropriate that we all review what was accomplished in 1968. Some of you accepted responsibility for group leadership, which surely contributed to Al-Anon's effectiveness. Others did much excellent Twelfth Step work, which increased Al-Anon's growth. Others made strides in personal understanding and practice of the program, which made them more valuable members.

You can look back with satisfaction on having done any or all of these things. But one fascinating and stimulating part of Al-Anon work is that you can bring new life and hope to someone in trouble or despair without realizing it. It sometimes is many months, even years, later that you learn you did help and how you did it.

Perhaps there's a letter in the FORUM which tells of new insight gained from a letter printed months before. You glow all over when you realize that that first letter was your own contribution. Perhaps just one person wrote in gratitude for the first letter; it's very possible, however, dozens of others got the same lift from it but didn't write.

Sometimes when you've given a talk at another group, and a year or so later when you meet a member of it, he tells that what you said in your talk enlightened him and spurred him on.

Again, you may make a brief comment at your own meeting and not know until much later that what you said was the first chink in a defensive member's armor, or a tightly closed mind until that moment, which led to his acceptance of the program.

When I think of this unknown reservoir of Al-Anon inspiration, it always reminds me of the early days at the Clearing House. Some days mail was heavy; forty or fifty letters answering cries for help were written and mailed. Occasionally there were only ten or a dozen. Lois invariably commented, as we prepared to go home, "Well, we got a lot done today, didn't we!"

We, just as invariably, teased her about her standard comment on our efforts. But all she'd do was smile her lovely, reasuring smile, and repeat, "We did get a lot done."

And the queer part is that she probably was exactly right. There was no way to tell which of the days did the most good. But there is utterly no question at all but that Lois' encouragement always helped, always inspired us to work a bit harder and to feel the great importance of that work. We felt wonderful.

So, in looking back over 1968, if you wish you had done more Twelfth Step work, had accepted a group office or any other responsibility you think you perhaps skimped on, remember Lois: you very likely got a lot done, a great part of which you may never know about.

And there's always 1969, in which you can work harder.

        Love and happy holidays to you.

"*Even the Desert Blooms*"

EVERYONE WHO KNOWS Lois knows her passionate love of flowers, plants, trees and everything to do with gardens. *Stepping Stones* well repays her tireless work in its beauty, simplicity and tranquility.

Thus it was not accidental that the analogy of working in a garden and working the Al-Anon program came to her when she wrote "BEFORE AL-ANON . . . Loneliness and Despair."

Over the years I have read it many times—back in the old days of the Clearing House (when it was titled "One Wife's Story), it was one of the only three pieces of literature we had. But then, as now, it did yeoman work for those who took the quarter-hour's time to read it.

Each time I read it, some new idea comes to me, something fresh and encouraging emerges to inspire me.

Reading it today, where she writes of different soils and how flowers can be grown in each, I found, "Even the desert blooms." Probably I've heard that sentence thirty or forty times. But only today did I realize the wisdom and comfort of it.

It impressed me now particularly because I've been thinking so constantly about a member of my group. She has hit a bad patch in recent weeks and in spite of a previous fine grasp and practice of Al-Anon principles, she finds herself depressed, questioning what she is putting into and getting out of Al-Anon.

As I listened to her, I knew she was totally unlike her usual self. As I heard her quickly sketch her recent activities, I knew why: she was tired to the bone but had been forcing herself to carry on as usual.

It was no wonder to me that something gave—something

had to: the stoutest of spirits occasionally flag. But when I read, "Even the desert blooms," I knew I had found comfort for my discouraged friend.

Think for a moment what that means. I've never seen a desert, in or out of bloom, just splendid pictures in the magazine, "Arizona Highways" which show a profusion of beautiful flowers, springing out of endless wastes of sand.

And remembering those glorious pictures, it came to me that we, too, have desert-places in our lives, just as my fellow-member has right now.

We don't know when our deserts will bloom, when the arid stretches will blossom into beauty. But we do know that as long as we are alive there is hope; trite but very true.

It may well be that we sometimes need these low spots in our lives; we cannot live at the peak always. As the desert needs rest and quiescence before it flames into bloom, just so may we need dormant periods to enable us to reach greater heights of understanding and acceptance.

If "Even the desert blooms," so can we. So can my dear friend.

Who Would Want to Be Infallible?

ONE OF THE GREATEST things about Al-Anon is the universality and common sense of its philosophy. One bit or another is almost sure-fire to straighten out any situation.

Take the Steps for instance. No one says they are easy to follow nor to be swallowed in one gulp. But, if you work at them conscientiously, give them due thought and make them an integral part of your life, you will be well-armed to face difficulties.

They teach you to work toward perfection, instead of assuming that you are perfect to begin with and have fallen into error through human perversity.

The Tenth Step is a good illustration. "Continued to take personal inventory and when we were wrong promptly admitted it." This Step does not say we have failed, even if we *have* failed miserably by making mistakes. It assumes that everyone does make mistakes occasionally and it implies that we begin to correct errors by recognizing them as such and by admitting them promptly.

All this was summed up quite succinctly for me the other day when I ran across a quotation—unfortunately the source wasn't given so I can't give credit. However the quote is a honey:

"The great may go wrong but they do not try to cover their tracks."

Could anything be more simple? Or more in keeping with the Al-Anon program? Or more comforting? It seems to say to you, "Surely the great are great, but even great people make mistakes. The only thing is that they don't ignore them, don't try to pretend they didn't make any."

Fortunately I live in a very normal family of human beings and I cannot think of any winged angels among them. I'm right at home with them and among my peers when I go wrong. Were they all perfect I'm sure I'd long since have been read out of the family and I believe I'd be as well content not to have to compete with absolute perfection!

The thing I have to remember is that I frequently do wrong things but that I can help to minimize those failings by admitting them, by not trying to pretend they never happened by covering them up.

That takes us straight back to Al-Anon's Tenth Step of

promptly admitting wrongs. It's certainly easier to blame another person, to think that he very likely provoked us into loss of control but it's not Al-Anon.

And when you think it all over, it seems to me it's a lot better to begin a little lower down and to rise higher through your own efforts than it is to start at the top and slide down through your own faults.

I don't believe I'd have lived this long, in my particular setting, if I were smugly perfect, infallibly right. No one could bear to have me around—they'd probably have extinguished me long since. And I could well understand that!

Always Tend to Your Own Knitting

MORE THAN a hundred years ago, in "Walden," Henry D. Thoreau wrote: "The mass of men lead lives of quiet desperation." Without doubt he was a true eccentric but his injunction, again in "Walden," to "Beware of all enterprises that require new clothes," always had endeared him to me and gave weight to what he wrote. I couldn't believe anyone who loved old clothes, as I do myself, could be very wrong.

On the principle that misery loves company, for many years I comforted myself with the thought that, indeed, most men do lead lives of quiet desperation. I was not unique, although my desperation was not always quiet.

Al-Anon's philosophy and program, when I really studied it deeply and accepted it, showed me that even so discerning a thinker as Thoreau could be wrong or at least hadn't thought far enough. I learned that there was no need and no excuse for desperation, quiet or otherwise.

I came to believe desperation stems from not being able to do anything constructive in a serious situation. Without Al-Anon's Family Group program I could only rebel futilely.

The thing which had driven me frantic was that I could see no good in and no excuse for the excessive and uncontrolled drinking. It upset our family relationships; played havoc with our finances, kept me on tenterhooks whether my husband was drinking or not and worst of all, he didn't even enjoy it!

I believe that last thought was what offended me most. My Scot's blood, generations back though it is, protested the extravagant waste of it. I really believe I could have borne it better, and suffered less, had he derived any pleasure from it.

You can see how far I was from realizing there was any compulsion about an alcoholic's drinking. Al-Anon, although it took me a long time to get it, did teach and help me.

I came to accept the fact of alcoholism as a disease, which only my husband could control. I came to believe that my part in our lives was to accept my own powerlessness over alcohol. Al-Anon taught me to concentrate my efforts on regaining my own serenity and making our family life as tranquil as I could.

Thoreau went on to say that "what is called resignation is confirmed desperation." I believe this. People say you should resign yourself to what you cannot change. Webster defines resign as surrender, quit, abandon, relinquish. All these are negative ideas, which I couldn't accomplish, so I did become desperate.

Al-Anon says, "Accept the things I cannot change." It was only with this acceptance that I began to come up, for what was practically the third time.

By accepting powerlessness, by admitting what was my own role and my own province, the desperation lessened and finally disappeared. Al-Anon taught me to tend to my own knitting and leave my husband to tend to his.

Serenity: Our Greatest Safeguard

"WHEN I FEEL the calm of my spirit has been broken by emotional upset, then I must steal away alone . . ." because "uncalm times are the only times when evil can find an entrance."

This is from a book my AA husband is so devoted to that he reads to me from it and we have what amounts to a short, private meeting.

This business of uncalm times leading to the entrance of evil seemed particularly apt to me because of a worrying situation in which I am at present involved. The emphasis on serenity in our program has always been, to me, one of the greatest values of all.

When I came to Al-Anon I was thoroughly sick and tired of the turmoil I had created for years within myself. I desperately wanted the serenity I saw in my fellow members but somehow could not acknowledge my powerlessness over alcohol. Always there was that stubborn hope I would somehow think up the perfect gimmick to entice my husband into sobriety. Only when it finally penetrated my resistant mind exactly where my responsibility—or capability—ended and his began, did I appreciate the futility of batting my spirit against something I could not change. Only then did a measure of serenity come and was reflected in our household. A truly blessed day!

At present I can see much of my old self in two wives,

both of whom I met through AA; one is in Al-Anon, the other not. Except that I never sought outside help, that I kept all my anger, resentment and despair at a rolling boil within myself, these two women are at present as unable to help themselves and their mates as I was. They keep trying, though, however misguidedly.

So far as I can tell, both husbands are making valiant efforts toward sobriety under difficult circumstances. And what circumstances aren't difficult in this problem? Tensions would certainly be lessened if the wives could somehow really practice the Serenity Prayer.

Instead, despite some months of abstinence by both spouses, if either is late ten minutes in arriving home, the wife immediately thinks the worst and is visibly upset when her husband gets home. Both are breath-sniffers, although what either could do if she got a whiff is beyond me.

Neither wife seems ever to relax; their phones are constantly busy with calls to friends, where complaints of past binges, fear of one beginning soon and dread of future ones is their main topic. It is all but impossible to get a word in.

None of this is good. Even the non-Al-Anon wife has been told enough of our program by now to know she is adding gigantic hazards to steady sobriety. Why, then, do they continue in so fruitless an effort?

They have, I believe, worked themselves into such a frenzy that they now cannot stop by themselves. Their "wrongs" occupy so large a part of their minds they can no longer listen to what is said—they just wait until the speaker pauses and then take up where they left off.

Do I believe either situation is hopeless, even though it sometimes surely seems so? No, I decidedly do not. Disheartening, yes; discouraging, yes, but hopeless, no. Too many miracles have occurred in Al-Anon and AA for me ever to despair of new ones. Sometime, some word most likely will open a crack in deaf ears. Some day an unexpected chink will let a small ray of light into the darkest place. And peace will come to them and to their husbands.

These are extreme cases. They developed from fear, upset and emotional uncontrol into practically major catastrophes. The only good I can see in either is that others of us may learn object lessons from them.

The very moment we feel "the calm of our spirit broken by emotional upset," that very moment we must make ourselves aware that evil can enter and we should steal away alone to regain serenity.

No Problem Is Without a Solution

A LETTER to the FORUM told of a problem a member found most disturbing. It didn't seem an insurmountable situation to us at all. But it did to the writer.

Esther B., Montclair, N.J., of the Editorial Board, commented in discussing it, "A very wise doctor said to me once that if something is a problem to you, it IS a problem and must be solved. Do not compare your problems with those of others."

That observation has recurred to me a dozen times since Esther tossed it out so lightly. In fact, I believe it is as good as a whole meeting if we just apply it thoughtfully.

It took me back to the most frustrating year of my life, out on the beautiful Montana ranch I had hoped to keep operating while my husband was with the 14th Air Force in China. I felt a great responsibility to him and to his partner. I also considered my running the ranch my special contribution to WW II: food production was vital; the country needed beef, pigs, turkeys, hay and grain.

The season was late; everything took longer to do because it was impossible to get adequate help—the hay crew was four, instead of a dozen. Grain was so late maturing there was great danger it would freeze as it stood.

I read government bulletins by lamplight, late into the night; I talked to the most successful ranchers in the valley to learn their shortcuts. They were generous in telling me how things should be best done under the circumstances. I would tactfully and confidently tell my "boys" how we could save time and work by doing what the J Bar L was going to do.

They would agree. But time after time they held to the way they and their fathers had done things in Nebraska, under very different circumstances. They privately agreed no fool woman's newfangled notions would change them.

Had I had Al-Anon's teaching then, I'd have accepted it as a thing I couldn't change, which is the solution I finally found. I was a little ashamed of it then. Many times I walked the floor in desperation; took my .22 to a pasture gophers were ruining and tried to wipe them out; many times I just sat sadly on a stump and looked at the mountains.

It was a very real problem. It did no good to get furious with them, to remind myself they had promised Jack they'd work for me as they would for him while he went to war. I wasn't happy with the solution but I'm sure now it was the only one in an impossible situation.

Very much earlier, at eight or nine, I'd found a satisfactory solution to a very important problem: I had been fitted for glasses and hated them. They were ruining my life, I thought. In less than two weeks I broke them three times. I'd take them to my father and say, quite truthfully,

"I broke my glasses." Since I played with boys a lot, Father probably thought it natural I'd have more difficulties with my glasses than my quiet older sister. He'd get them repaired.

Breaking the glasses solved nothing; they just got mended, so I put my mind on the problem: I went out to a large marshy place, shut my eyes, whirled them around my head and let go. That night, when asked where they were, I said, again truthfully if deceitfully, "I don't know—they're lost."

With that my father gave up. I'm sure I couldn't have needed them badly as it wasn't until college, when horn-rims were fashionable, that I asked for some. Very likely there was a better solution than the one I found but I did find a solution.

In Al-Anon my greatest problem was the First Step. I fought it for years and years, thus complicating the whole problem for myself and my family. I knew others accepted it almost immediately but it continued to be a problem to me.

Then, after years, in what I'm sure was a spiritual awakening, it suddenly flashed upon me that I actually WAS powerless over alcohol. That made sense and that problem was solved.

So, if you have a problem, big or small, think it through until you find the solution you can accept. Don't panic. Don't think in circles. When you find yourself protesting against the problem, haul your mind off the protest and put it back to hunting for a sensible solution.

There's always one if you look hard enough.

Use Al-Anon's Armor to Combat Useless Fear

FEAR UNDOUBTEDLY has its uses: children must be taught to fear strange bottles lest they swallow poison. Fear drives us to seek help from competent doctors lest we develop serious disorders. Fear is sometimes a valuable warning device. But also it frequently is a rot, as the poet Robert Graves says.

This kind of fear, this rot, is the kind which harms so many in our fellowship. They come to groups so fear-ridden they cannot, at first, accept the offered enlightenment. They are so steeped in apprehensions they cannot listen attentively. Their minds continually stray and jump from one anxiety to another, more dire than the first.

Years ago, someone sent the FORUM a wonderful Stopper: "Fear knocked at the door. Faith answered. And lo, there was no one there!" It has been quoted in several of my articles since then. Many members have re-submitted it, not knowing or remembering it had already been printed. But with Al-Anon's constantly increasing membership, this stimulating little precept, admonition, exhortation—call it what you will—merits as frequent repetition as the Serenity Prayer.

So much of Al-Anon's philosophy is packed into those short sentences—so easily remembered—that they constantly come to mind when I'm doing Twelfth Step work.

Fear has knocked at so many of our doors, both before and after we first came to Al-Anon, there's little need to expand the point. We actually lived in a welter of fears, big and small, unable to cope with them.

Gradually, as Al-Anon's teachings began to penetrate our fog, we gained a little hope and an assurance that things could probably never be half as bad as we feared.

We gained enough faith actually to examine our fears and to face them.

When we did face them, we realized that many were bogeymen, figments of our own imaginations. Frequently they never materialized. Many of Al-Anon's slogans bear on this subject:

- Easy Does It—don't knock yourself out, fearing what probably isn't there.
- Let Go and Let God—you can't have everything to suit yourself but never fear, your Higher Power will help you cope.
- Twenty-four Hours a Day—concentrate on just this moment and not on the fear of what might, but hasn't yet, happened.
- First Things First—you can never gain the serenity you seek if you dissipate your strength in nameless fears.
- Live and Let Live—your life is too important to you and to others for you to spend it in a turmoil of fear. Live it confidently and don't penalize those around you by making them live with a craven shell of yourself.

"Fear knocked at the door. Faith answered. And lo, there was no one there!" There's a lot of meaning packed into those few words. You'll find new meanings every time you give them a little thought. They are a very valuable part of Al-Anon's arsenal against slips.

Al-Anon's Program Enlightens the World

STRAY GLIMPSES of long-familiar sights sometimes have a most unusual effect. They stimulate new insights, give new inspiration, new determination to try harder to do a job which occasionally has become routine.

A sketch of the Statue of Liberty jolted me recently. I've seen her dozens of times, from the deck of a ship and from the air. From the air she's never been particularly impressive—just a sort of identification I'm on my way West somewhere.

But from shipboard there's always been a catch in my throat, a wonderment of what she must mean to the thousands of immigrants who see her as evidence of a dream come true.

The drawing was just part of an ad, with a quote from the poem on the pedestal: "Give me your tired, your poor, your huddled masses yearning to breathe free . . . Send these . . . to me: I lift my lamp beside the golden door."

As I looked at the sketch I suddenly felt it was Al-Anon standing there, instead of a woman with a crown on her head, a torch in one hand, a book in the other. I saw a different symbolism in it. I saw the spirit of Al-Anon going out to the whole world, ready and eager to share its blessings of healing, hope and knowledge with anyone in need.

Not everyone who enters Liberty's golden door finds a perfect life. Perhaps some seek an unreasonable dream. But surely no one ever sought in vain, for relief from intolerable burdens, in Al-Anon, if he honestly tried to follow its precepts. It is perfectly true that not all who come to Al-Anon stay with it. Occasionally even established members drop out.

In such cases, it seems to me, there is an unwillingness to give up, an inability to keep an open mind, a rejection of some important part of the program which accounts for the failure.

"Principles above personalities" is difficult for those who have always allowed themselves to indulge in personal likes and dislikes in judging actions. Some find it difficult to subordinate themselves and their wishes to the common good of the Al-Anon group. Some are content to listen, more or less perfunctorily, to Al-Anon's teachings and leave it at that.

But to those who are eager to know and to understand exactly how and why they should change old ways, Al-Anon's lamp can shine through any door. We all were tired, poor. We huddled, not in masses usually, but miserably within ourselves. Above all, we yearned to "breathe free." In desperation we came to Al-Anon.

Many of us found there a ray of hope when we learned that an illness, not wanton self-indulgence, willfulness nor shameful selfishness caused the situation which made us so unhappy. We began to realize our responsibility for our share in making that situation worse. We learned that even if we could not change the situation, we could accept it and live with it.

Once our own burden has been lifted or lightened by the gifts Al-Anon has bestowed, in return for our following its program, we are able to "breathe free." We are able to think of others and, above everything else, to share those gifts with others who still live in the darkness which once encompassed us.

Al-Anon must be boundless while there is one case of alcoholism still not arrested. Part of its glory is the inspiration it gives most of us to share its blessings. Passing on to others the benefits we have ourselves gained is our repayment for restored hope and happiness.

Twelfth Step work is, and should be, endless.

Al-Anon is Not a Sometime Thing

PEOPLE OFTEN ASK me why long-timers remain in our program. Surely, they say, after 15 to 20 years, there can't be much that is new in it for them—much to be learned about it.

The basics of the program are said to be very simple. They probably could be learned in a few meetings: alcoholism is an incurable illness and is primarily the alcoholic's business; we have no control over alcohol; our responsibility and our field of endeavor is within ourselves and with families of alcoholics; we can attain serenity even though the problem remains active; we can learn to live with dignity and quiet content, without letting alcoholic excess overwhelm us; we have just today in which to work; our goal is spiritual growth through the constant practice of the Twelve Steps; our obligation to the Al-Anon Family Groups is through a thorough understanding and faithful practice of the Twelve Traditions. There may even be something I have skipped in this quick summing up.

Now there may be some people who can master these "simple" principles, once and for all. But if so, I definitely am not among them.

It's true that in grade school arithmetic I once learned the multiplication tables—at least up to the "nine times . . ." table. I'm still unreliable there. And please don't tell me they're the easiest as the product always adds up to nine itself; that just adds another confusion factor for me. I still know those tables cold. But the Al-Anon program is entirely different.

Just take the Steps and the Serenity Prayer, for instance. I need to work on them constantly. The First Step and the first sentence of the Prayer are like Siamese Twins: inseparably joined, as far as I am concerned. They are connected, not just with alcohol but with many other situations in which I find myself. I need to examine each hurdle as it comes along to see if it is something over which I am powerless or if it is something I can change. I also need to gauge whether it could make my life unmanageable.

The decision to let God's will prevail is another fertile field for constant work. And the practice of these principles in all my affairs is not like learning multiplication tables. Without the constant reminders of active Al-Anon work I'm sure I'd honor a lot of them more "in the breach than the observance."

I don't believe I'm overly stupid nor self-willed. But I do believe I need frequent nudges. I get them from our Al-Anon program.

No human life has ever been perfect but Al-Anon can show me how to profit from the imperfections, rather than wasting time and energy in damaging resentments. Others may not need this reminder. But I do.

It is possible that some people have minds which are stocked and stored with all manner of information and resources, neatly assorted like books on library shelves.

Perhaps if I knew some of those people the temptation to abolish them would be strong, because my mind is a hodge-podge of assorted ideas based upon appealing bits picked up from here, there and everywhere. I never quite know what stimulus is going to set something boiling up, what bit will float to the surface from the disorderly depths.

But I've lived with that disorder a long time. I've constantly added new gems to it. And Al-Anon helps me haul them out when I need them. No one should ever "graduate" from Al-Anon. I'm afraid that if I ever tried to graduate myself from the program, everything would sink into a useless mess.

The shiningest bits I've added in the past 17 or 18 years have come, almost in toto, from Al-Anon. Take Barbara T's letter about resentments in this month's Answering Service. If I had graduated myself a month or two ago, I'd never have known the fundamental reason why I always pray immediately for someone who has hurt or annoyed me.

I've done it usually to get my mind off the hurt. But I now understand from her letter that it comes from an unconscious recognition of brotherhood. If any utter stranger provoked me, I'd brush it off instinctively. But as Barbara wrote, "God loves him just as much as He does me, is in him as much as in me," so I toss off a quick prayer for someone who is really my brother and feel calm again.

The more I think of what Al-Anon does for everyone who is wise enough to follow the program, the less I understand anyone dropping out or neglecting it. To me, it's a chance-of-a-lifetime, for-a-lifetime philosophy.

Al-Anons are Modern Alchemists

AL-ANON Twelfth Step work sometimes does not seem as dramatic as that of AA. I look among our friends and see men whom my husband Twelfth Stepped twenty, ten, five or three years ago. When I think they have not had a drink in all those years I occasionally wonder how my Al-Anon work stacks up beside his. And that is daft. There are far better ways for me to spend my time.

Al-Anon Twelfth Step work is quite as essential as that of AA. If that of AA successfully brings sobriety to the alcoholic, that of Al-Anon restores mental sobriety to whole families. Even though they had not been physically drunk, most of their lives had been as greatly out of control and as unmanageable as though they too had suffered from the disease of alcoholism.

Changes usually come more slowly in Al-Anon than in AA and, as said before, they don't seem as dramatic. When a drunk stops drinking, when he wholeheartedly accepts AA, he stops a lot of other things which used to make him stand out from his fellowmen. Even those who had been uncontrolled drinkers for twenty or thirty years seem able to take up life again with confidence and courage.

Courage, I believe, returns more slowly to the non-alcoholic partners. Perhaps because they have for so long a time built their lives and their outlook around their alcoholic mates—have been happy when there was a break in the drinking, sad when it was renewed—they now fear to believe that sobriety will endure.

However they do at last realize they do not control, and never have controlled, the alcoholic problem. They learn to put that problem back into the hands where it always had belonged: the Higher Power's and the alcoholic's. But to overcome their edginess, mistrust and inability to relax requires considerable time.

With Al-Anon's help they regain the ability to relax. They lose their mistrust and edginess little by little. They begin to enjoy life anew, rejoin the human race they have shut out for so long. They take up relationships and occupations long abandoned.

Fairly soon they learn to recognize in newcomers the need they themselves once suffered. They know what needs to be done and they are able to stretch out their willing hands to do it.

Let no one say that "the years of the locust" were extravagantly wasted ones, as I once considered them. Alchemists of the Middle Ages spent their whole lives futilely trying to turn base metals into gold. But through Al-Anon we have learned how to turn the dross of unhappy, rebellious years into the living gold of happiness, peace, serenity and hope . . . not just for ourselves but for all who seek help.

Speak to Newcomers in Their Own Language

ONE OF Al-Anon's greatest strengths is the ability to identify properly with fellow members. And it is not a "misery-loves-company" sort of thing, either.

All but a fortunate few come to their first meeting in desperation. Suffering under the old idea that excessive drinking was a disgrace, ignorant that it is an illness, most newcomers have imprisoned themselves behind high, strong walls which not only shut them in but keep all others out. They are their own jailers.

Families, friends and neighbors were kept at arm's length lest they stumble upon what we considered our "shameful secret." Some of these newcomers, it is true, had cast dignity to the winds and everlastingly complained about their suffering to anyone who'd listen. They had not realized that understanding was needed, not the weakening sympathy, generously extended to them in error.

Both kinds of sufferers—the strong (?), silent ones and the vociferous complainers—come to Al-Anon in equal need of help.

I was the silent type. I buried my head deeper in the sand than an ostrich. I fooled only myself. I'd had several years of fine AA meetings which, if misery-loving-company is an answer, had failed me completely. I had learned that many others faced the same situation but it hadn't done me much good.

Then came Al-Anon. I was slow to learn even in it but I did immediately feel there were answers for me and it was up to me to find them. I knew Al-Anon was meant for me and for my problems, just as AA was meant for the alcoholic. That was the first great surge toward freedom.

I remember the first time, years and years ago, that I put

Al-Anon to work and risked a slight breach in my hitherto impenetrable wall. We had recently moved. A dearly loved neighbor, just widowed, phoned to say she was going abroad. She was to be in town that afternoon only and would like to come to say goodbye. Naturally I asked her to tea and prepared an impressive one.

Then at noon the blow fell. My husband came home unexpectedly, the worse for wear. He'd seemed all right at breakfast—and I was frantic. Our apartment was about the size of two card-tables; the walls were tissue thin and I could think of no way to reach Dorothy to stop her coming, which was my first impulse. The lovely sandwiches, fancy petits fours, jumbo salted nuts, all mocked me during the ages I waited for her ring.

Then, like the Marines in the movies, as I watched her come up the stairs, Al-Anon came to my rescue. I'd attended only a few meetings but I had learned courage to face the situation.

As she moved toward the bedroom with her hat and coat, I said lightly, "Better bring them here. The body is lying in state in there and he's best not disturbed."

"I'm sorry," she said. "Why didn't you tell me he's sick and I wouldn't have bothered you." "I'm not bothered," I said. "He reunioned with his old outfit last night and celebrated too well. He's just got a hangover—he earned it. I stayed home alone and I'm feeling fine." And I was, suddenly.

She just laughed and said what an unsympathetic, hardboiled Hannah I was and went on to tell how she'd once overindulged and how she suffered. I completely relaxed. No moan or groan from the bedroom upset either of us.

Long before, I thought I had accepted alcoholism as an illness but I very evidently had never accepted the compulsion of it. I'd given it lip-service only.

Newcomers ask why alcoholics drink when they really don't want to, when they know how one drink will inevitably lead to trouble, when they know all the answers and actually long for sobriety. That question still bothers me a little. I now know it is because of compulsion; that they have not yet substituted an equal compulsion against drinking. But since I have whole-heartedly accepted my powerlessness over alcohol, I have further accepted the fact that following the AA program is the alcoholic's business, not mine, and that is the answer I make to newcomers.

I can identify with these troubled newcomers because I once agonized over the same difficulties. They identify with me because they recognize their mistakes when I tell them mine.

Al-Anon is like speaking a language. Even though handling alcoholic problems is not native to our previous experience, through the program we have learned how to meet situations, just as we learn fluency in a foreign tongue.

Al-Anon members have a common bond of experience which brings understanding and enables us to offer help, hope and restored joy in living to those who come to us in despair. We not only speak their language, we have made ourselves bilingual in the alcoholic and non-alcoholic worlds. We should keep fluent.

Thank God for Al-Anon.

Al-Anon's Program Comes to the Rescue

SOMETIMES my mind does such queer things I begin to question if I really have one. After all the years of Al-Anon, you'd think there'd be no possibility of a negative thought finding houseroom in it, even momentarily.

Such thoughts nevertheless do creep in. Just a month or so ago I shocked myself. True, we had a winter and spring which shouldn't have happened to a dog.

Jack and I had played pat-ball with flu germs so that one or the other was always either coming down with a new go at it or just recuperating from one. Then I followed with a most annoying ear infection, better forgotten now. Just as we began to relax and felt half-human again, our daughter became gravely ill and was hospitalized nearly three months.

Anyhow, the day I shocked myself I was reading the Psalms. Attentively—I thought. But I came upon, "For I alone am afflicted." Further on, something kept nagging at me. I stopped reading, thought a minute and said to myself, "Something's wrong. These are Psalms I'm reading—David, not Job." So I turned back the pages and re-read, correctly this time, "For I am alone and afflicted."

That may not seem as startling to you as it did to me. But to me, "I alone" is the quintessence of self-pity. To some, "Alone and afflicted" may seem to lean a bit to the self-pitying side but not to me. It's just a factual, dispassionate summing-up.

I was amazed and upset that I had subconsciously switched the words around because I hadn't realized I had allowed myself to sink so low. When things were at their worst, in years past, I never indulged in that "poor little me" attitude I always found disgusting. To begin with, I'm not little. Neither have I ever felt that I have been unduly put upon—in fact I have always felt I probably have been blessed beyond my deserts.

But there it was: "I alone," as if I'd been singled out from all others for affliction! That ended the Psalms for that day. I don't know whether I spent the next half hour on the Tenth or the Eleventh Step—I believe it was a combination of both.

I mentally reviewed the past winter and spring in detail. I decided I was physically at a low ebb from illness, that I was not seeing things in proper perspective. I was rebelling at my daughter's illness instead of concentrating on thanking God she was recovering.

The various parts of the program fell into place: I could see where and how I had gone wrong. I had been placing my own will above that of God and, powerless over carrying out either mine or His, I had landed in a mess.

But a wonderful part of Al-Anon's philosophy is that there is always something to be done if you are willing to work at it. Once I realized I had slipped into the trap of self-pity, I could pull up my socks and stop it immediately. I had only to look about me to see how really fortunate I was. I could stop regretting what had happened and begin to be grateful it hadn't been worse.

I could stop putting my will above God's and begin again, more wholeheartedly, to pray for the power to carry out His. I could work harder at "practicing these principles in all my affairs."

People sometimes just coast along, riding on momentum. I believe that's what I had been doing. Not from smugness, I hope; probably more a case of just taking Al-Anon for granted. It took the simple fact of mixing up the order of a few words to shake me out of that complacency. I'm glad I mixed them up. Straightening them out helped straighten me out.

We in Al-Anon Have Priceless Gifts to Give

TO MANY PEOPLE, Christmas is a day of giving and of sharing, a heart-warming day of childhood recollections, remembrance of old friends and new, of loving thoughts and wishes for everyone the world over.

We in the Al-Anon Family Group fellowship are among the most fortunate of Earth's creatures because our giving is spread throughout the entire year when we practice our program in all our daily affairs. And we always have priceless gifts to give: restored hope, renewed faith and unselfish love.

Occasionally human frailty traps us into wondering if we really can help others when we have made so many mistakes ourselves. Here Longfellow may give you the lift he did me. Not long ago I happened upon a couple of lines where he said, "Give what you have. To some one, it may be better than you dare to think."

I was preparing a talk to give at a large, very important meeting of Al-Anons and AAs. I wanted to do an outstanding job, worthy of their confidence in inviting me. The theme of the entire day was Recovery Through Knowledge and mine was to be a personal recovery story to close the program.

Naturally I began with the "How sick I was" part—the state from which I recovered through Al-Anon's program. As I jotted down the mistaken things I had done, one sillier than another, some amusing, some tragically burdensome to me, all of them misguided and hurtful, the thought crossed my mind as it has so many times before, "These things you did were so stupid, you fought the First Step so long and so stubbornly, perhaps they'll think you are not worth listening to, that anyone so far off base couldn't recover."

But what could I do? I had done those things and couldn't deny it. They were all I had to tell to point up what I like to think is the recovery I have made. As the song goes, "I've come a long way, Baby!" And I believe I really have helped some people over the years.

It was as I was reviewing my failures that I remembered Longfellow's "It may be better than you dare to think."

Thus I was able to ignore my regret for such a silly, stupid story as mine before the Al-Anon program really changed my life. I concentrated on what had given me the courage and knowledge to overcome my stubborn persistence in errors.

And so I gave my talk. Longfellow was right. I gave what I had and it was better than I had dared to hope, if those who thanked me afterwards weren't just being kind. They said I had shown them mistakes they still were making and had pointed the way to recovery.

The very fact that I had continued so long and so obstinately to mismanage my life, that I had allowed myself to become an utter recluse and yet now could talk to four hundred or more people, gave them hope. They knew that if I could do it, they could. Through Al-Anon, they can.

All of which brings me back to what we of Al-Anon have to give and to share. We can celebrate Christmas every day. We may not have wealth nor material gifts to shower upon others. But we do have the wisdom gained from dearly-bought experience with which to encourage others.

Every day and every person seeking Al-Anon's teachings, is our opportunity to make Christmas last throughout the year. Our gift to all who come to us for help in living with an alcoholic problem is a gift above rubies. In making it we become part of an Al-Anon chain which links the world.

And so, as always, my wish for you is that every holiday joy be yours and may Al-Anon strengthen and guide you all through the year.

Putting the Past to Work for Others

ONE TWO-EDGED facet of life today is the incredible speed of communication. News, good and bad, flashes around the world instantly. Seemingly, at times, most of it is grim.

If we allow ourselves to dwell exclusively upon bad news, we are headed for trouble. That would be like casting up a balance sheet where we counted only the slow-selling merchandise remaining on the shelves, without taking credit for what had been sold profitably.

Perhaps there is little or nothing we can do about some of the events which make us unhappy. But to offset those, we can always remember there is one field in which we are well-experienced, where we can do much to make life happier and easier—for others.

We can now look back upon times when we rebelled at what we then considered an extravagant waste of time and talent. We thought that waste was caused by wanton self-indulgence on the part of our loved one. What turned the screw most tightly, what we found most unforgivable, was that the drinker did not even enjoy the drinking.

That was how many of us were before we embraced the Al-Anon philosophy. But we can see now that every unhappy incident was only a step in the training we needed to mature. Once we learned that alcoholism is an illness, not a positive proof of rejection of our love and concern, we were able to move out of the high and mighty judgment seats in which we had coldly installed ourselves.

We could accept that past experience, not as something visited upon us to bedevil us, but as something to make us grow. Through the success we achieved in applying Al-Anon's program, we were able to stretch out life-saving hands to others still rebelling.

And from the first successful Twelfth Step job we accomplished, we saw our former life in different perspective. It ceased to be an unhappy waste and we came to recognize it as a time of preparation. Without it we would be ill-prepared to help newcomers. We'd be as misguided as the doctor to whom I went for help many years ago. He advised, in well-meant ignorance, that my husband take two drinks every night before dinner. He believed such a practice would solve the problem.

Two things we should do to help others: we should care and we should share. If we accepted all of Al-Anon's blessings as our right, and stopped there, we didn't make the program our own. So long as we know of one person in need of our help, we should not be content to stand idly by.

We have vast experience behind us. Some of it may be exactly what another needs. Al-Anon's teachings showed us how to transmute personal tragedy into strengths which enable us to guide others to the same success. We moved from unhappy darkness into the cheering light of full day with Al-Anon's aid. We ended futile rebellion at every exasperating trifle. We gathered courage and a will to live in ever-increasing serenity and helpfulness.

This is the first month of a whole new year. Let us strive to put our past to work for others in the best, most helpful way we can, every month of this year. Let's make 1970's Twelfth Step work our best yet. Thus, as we have emerged victors in our fight against the past, that success can lead others to the same triumphant outcome.

Anger can be Friend as well as Foe

LONG BEFORE the Sermon on the Mount promised that "the meek shall inherit the earth," an early Psalm advised: "Cease from anger, and forsake wrath . . . the meek shall inherit the earth; and shall delight themselves in the abundance of peace."

It's nice to know that the meek will be lavishly rewarded some day but I've always felt that meekness isn't always everything. I know for a fact that quite a number of angry men have helped to improve the real estate the meek will inherit.

When enough people got angry enough at the widespread air and water pollution in "America the Beautiful," a movement began to clear it up. When greedy lumber companies threatened huge areas of land by denuding them of trees, angry men enforced programs of scientific harvesting and replanting. Even wildlife benefited. Whooping cranes were nearly extinct until angry men took steps to have them protected. Today their numbers, while still small, have greatly increased so that our children's children may still catch a glimpse of them one day.

Angry men and women have a definite place, and a job to do, even in some Al-Anon groups. They don't necessarily make bad friends in clearing up bad situations which threaten group-unity. They do need, usually, to persevere.

Some groups have been unhappy because a Mr. or a Mrs. Al-Anon felt, and took, too great a part in management; permitted no other voice to be heard, no plans to be carried out but their own. Sometimes concerned members could straighten out such situations. Sometimes a group had to be broken up and re-formed into a new, more democratic one.

Then there have been groups which permitted too much talk of spouses until it really amounted to gossip. Wiser heads among them, angry, appalled, concerned—call it what you will—feared that such perversion of Al-Anon's meetings was dangerous to Al-Anon and AA. They determined to replace such loose talk by confining discussions exclusively to Al-Anon's program. They persisted until Al-Anon meetings became real Al-Anon meetings.

Still other members found groups too complacent, provincial and much too preoccupied with local problems. They were stimulated enough by indignation at such limitation of the Al-Anon program that they quietly, gradually, worked to enlarge the groups' horizons until most of them could appreciate their own place in a larger, wider world.

Anger needn't be loud shouting, uncontrolled tirades at another's fault nor unbridled scene-making. It can be a stimulous to better things, a helpful tool for cleaning up bad situations, an energy-producer when it is properly directed.

I believe there is a place for anger in Al-Anon specifically, as well as in the world at large. Temper tantrums are childish exhibitions which should neither be permitted nor confused with good healthy anger. Righteous anger makes all go out and conquer obstacles to Al-Anon's growth and welfare.

Discussion of the Serenity Prayer—Part I

"GOD GRANT ME THE SERENITY TO ACCEPT THE THINGS I CANNOT CHANGE."

By the time we came to Al-Anon, serenity was something we perhaps once had, a word in the dictionary or an item in the newspaper. It gradually had been lost and replaced with a bitter determination to change that "souse" we lived with into a spouse.

Sometimes we did change things. I did, frequently. By staunch opposition I frequently changed a passing idea of a drink into a solid determination to have ten. By thrusting AA on my husband, I lessened its effectiveness—AA is for AAs and they prefer it straight, not filtered through non-alcoholics, ignorant ones at that.

Then came Al-Anon. We saw serenity in action. The first time I found myself laughing when a newcomer said in horror that "He hides bottles," I knew I was on the right road. My life had been a prolonged game of Hide and Seek, when I'd hunt out the bottles he'd hidden so that I could hide them from him. I wasn't playing for fun. Nor did I have it. I was just grim Nemesis.

When told that alcoholism is the alcoholic's problem and only he can solve it, I had to do serious thinking, to weigh just what success had ever come from my efforts to solve the problem. Honesty compelled the admission I had never helped, just added to the difficulties. When told the problem was his, that mine was the problem of how to accept and live with it, a gleam of light shone.

It was only necessary to look back upon the turmoil and frantic disorder in which I had lived, to know that Al-Anon made sense. I recognized that walking the floor in agony until four-thirty in the morning had only exhausted me, until I was too tired and too disturbed to cope with *any* situation. Letting the phone ring because I was afraid to answer it, only frayed my nerves until I was a wreck. Stealing his money hadn't kept him from getting more and it only maddened him and sickened me.

Certainly changes were due and overdue. Those I had made heretofore hadn't pleased me. Al-Anon showed me a whole new world to conquer—right under my own hair, nice and handy!

Once an intelligent person recognizes the stupidity of persisting in useless, wasteful, actually-harmful behavior, there is hope for improvement. Decent sleep helped to an improved disposition; the answered phone frequently was a wrong number, not the police, hospital or employer. I once again began to be human. Serenity did not come overnight—but neither had I lost it overnight.

Serenity did come, however, and it did teach me to distinguish between the things I could change and those I could not. It showed me where to put my efforts. And it paid off—going in circles is much more exhausting than hewing to a line which gets one forward!

Discussion of the Serenity Prayer—Part II

"THE COURAGE TO CHANGE THE THINGS I CAN"

One of the greatest blessings of Al-Anon, to me, is that it gives direction to our lives. All too often, for too long a time, we had passively accepted whatever came, fighting back against whatever hurt us with nagging complaints and shrewish behavior. Neither approach had been effective—each had added unpleasantness to an already unpleasant situation. We had reacted against the stabs but we did nothing positive about them.

Everybody had lost: nagging the alcoholic had confirmed him in his determination to continue drinking. The scenes we created stirred up the family and kept them stirred. We, ourselves, had deteriorated both physically and morally by our lapse of self-control.

Then came Al-Anon, teaching us that alcoholism was the alcoholic's problem, which we could not solve for him. But we could work on our acceptance of the problem, could work on our own reactions to it and could make ourselves calmer, wiser persons to live with and to direct our homes and families.

From being hagridden by all manner of fears, both big and little, Al-Anon showed us how to regain control. It showed us that almost anything we did was an improvement. Thus encouraged, we could go on. It taught us to begin with something small, like walking out on a maudlin argument instead of remaining to add our share to the dispute and thus aggravate the situation. It taught us not to walk the floor all night but to go to bed so that the next day we were better able to cope.

In a word, Al-Anon gave us hope. And with hope, we had an impulse toward bettering ourselves. We began to see the things we could not change but God gave us courage to begin changing those we could. With success in changing the small things, our courage grew so that we could attack those more important. Our lives began to straighten out. We prayed for courage to change what we could and directed our energies toward that—we stopped drifting and began aiming, and working, toward an orderly, useful life.

Discussion of the Serenity Prayer—Part III

"AND THE WISDOM TO KNOW THE DIFFERENCE."

There is a great comfort in the thought that wisdom can be attained by all manner of persons. One needn't go to a great university to search for it. Inherent in a fortunate few, the rest of us can achieve a reasonable degree of wisdom if we give ourselves a chance.

I remember an old neighbor in Montana who was wise—

yet she could neither read nor write. She taught me a lot. One spring the ranch boys brought Marggy a newly-born pig. The sow had too many to cope with and they thought we'd like to try. Marggy was five and enchanted. But piglets weren't meant for humans to raise. This one quickly died. I was in a quiet dither. Marggy had never seen death and I was at a loss to make her understand, to soften the blow.

Fortunately old Annie was there; she took over. She got Marggy a box, set her to gathering moss and wild flowers and pretty stones for a grave. All the time she talked of a pig-heaven and how lovely the little pig looked. Marggy was left with no scar from that first encounter with death, thanks to the instinctive wisdom of our unlettered friend.

I have often been grateful to Annie for this and for the other things she unconsciously taught me of ways to handle difficult situations. All too often, it seems to me, we give up too easily. We say we can't do thus and so because we don't know how to go about it. But if we *want* it enough, I believe we can get the needed wisdom through this prayer. We'll never get it by flying off the handle when something displeases us. We'll never get it if we always talk and never think. We'll never get it through the care and feeding of grudges. Nor through fear.

But anybody can build upon the inherent good born in all of us. By thoughtful and prayerful consideration of what troubles us, we can find the wise way out. We can determine what is best for everyone if we forget ourselves: my own fear of Marggy's being hurt by Piglet's death confused me—Annie thought only of Marggy and what would help her.

When we have attained even a modicum of wisdom, that little bit will show us which things we can change, which we can't and should never even try to alter.

But for the Grace of God

THIS SLOGAN, I BELIEVE, is used more by AAs than by Al-Anons. An AA friend told me she used it on every Twelfth Step call she ever made. No matter in what stage she found the person, "But for the Grace of God" still was useful: if the woman was close to DTs, Nancy thanked God for her own sobriety which had brought her past that danger point; if the woman was resentful, Nancy thanked God for the serenity which had helped her overcome her own resentments, from which, but for the Grace of God, she might still be suffering.

When this slogan does come up in Al-Anon, it is usually brought to our attention by someone who is acute enough, and detached enough to recognize how accidental this whole business of alcoholism is. Any one of us might have been the alcoholic, but for the Grace of God, since alcoholism is an illness. In my rebellion against compulsive drinking I used to protest, swear it would have been better had I been the alcoholic in our family. Long ago, Al-Anon taught me what I should have known before, that God knows better than I.

As a non-alcoholic, I have been spared the unbearable remorse, the killing sense of guilt, the self-loathing that alcoholics suffer until they make peace with themselves in AA. But for the Grace of God, the lightning could have struck me, rather than my husband.

Thus, if any trace of smugness remains in any of us when we see some wretched creature struggling with his affliction, let's pause a moment and remember, "But for the Grace of God, there go I." From the uproar we managed to create just living with the problem, let's contemplate the hell we'd have raised with the problem itself. I'm sure God knew his business when he made me the Al-Anon, not the alcoholic. I thank Him and I hope I never forget to be grateful.

Al-Anon's "Three Important Days"

LIKE GAUL, DIVIDED in three parts, Time is divided into the past, the present and the future—Yesterday, Today and Tomorrow.

In Al-Anon you frequently hear that Yesterday is gone and nothing can be done about it. That's almost true—you can't change what actually happened. But you certainly can change your thinking about it. If someone did you an incomprehensible hurt, instead of nursing a grudge forevermore, you can put yourself in the other's place, sort out what made him do it and, through understanding, heal that hurt. Yesterday does have a place in showing you how best to live Today.

Tomorrow is a different matter. It is out of your hands, except as you too try to prepare to make the best use of it. You can no more live in the future than you can in the past. If you've made a mess of Today, you can just hope there'll be another day when you can do better. You can determine to do better and work on that.

Today—this very moment—is all you are sure of. And that flashing instant has gone to join the past even before you are aware of it. With this dizzy spin of Time the only safe way to make each moment count is to make our Al-Anon program so much an integral part of you that right responses are habitual—you can't go wrong following Al-Anon's teaching. With them, there's no regret for Yesterday. There's guidance for Today and hope for Tomorrow.

The Lord's Prayer

IT'S A GOOD THING Al-Anon and AA don't have to choose between the two prayers most closely associated with them—the Lord's Prayer and the Serenity Prayer. Each contains fundamentals of the program.

Just as we close each meeting with the Lord's Prayer, it seems very appropriate that we close the FORUM year with a consideration of how it fits into our program. AA took its program in bits and pieces from here, there and almost everywhere. Al-Anon, in turn, took its program from AA, unashamedly borrowing, adapting where necessary which was not often, and went forward from there.

The unity of Al-Anon is well expressed where we all acknowledge a common Father. The concept of His power is indicated when we place Him in heaven, well above our mortal effort. Our goal of being restored to sanity is in the words "Thy kingdom come" because the mess we once made of our lives was surely not to His liking.

We express the Third Step in almost the same words when we say "Thy will be done on earth as it is in Heaven." And asking for our daily bread—not food for a whole lifetime, not for next year nor next month, but for our daily bread—couldn't be closer to the 24 hour program. Then we can hardly ask forgiveness for trespasses we don't acknowledge as wrongs, so the moral inventory is implied there.

Finally, the Eleventh Step is certainly close to our petition that we not be led into temptation but delivered from evil, because we know His will for us could not be that of continued wrongdoing.

In one way or another, a tremendous part of our program is contained in the Lord's Prayer. One can hear and feel a special plea when it is said together in meetings. Any prayer is a good prayer but this one, peculiarly adapted to our needs, is our best one.

Listen and Learn!

DURING THE YEAR we plan to discuss what might be called valiant adjuncts to our basic guides, the Steps and Traditions. We'll discuss not only the slogans but what may well become slogans some time.

Since this is the beginning of a new year it seems appropriate to begin with a new precept: LISTEN AND LEARN! Whether we were driven to Al-Anon or came along willingly, we did come and we learned, so we can take the second part for granted. But some of us have difficulty with the first: LISTEN. We can learn faster if we listen properly.

Some time ago a woman came to our group so resentful of her son's behavior that she could speak of nothing else: she had done everything for him—paid his debts, bought his clothes, given him money (he was in his mid-forties) and put up with his uncontrolled drinking. And now, in payment for all her love and care, he'd taken up with *"Some Woman!"*

We thought her visit was her first exposure to Al-Anon; to our amazement we learned she'd attended many meetings years ago. Although she said she came for help—it was evident she needed it badly—she never stopped talking long enough to listen to any suggestion.

Every member of the group tried to help her. She talked everyone down and left the meeting a bit more confirmed in her conviction that she was a helpless victim of unmitigated selfishness. Had she listened, even a moment, windows of hope would have been opened to her; she'd have learned how best to cope with her own problems and even, perhaps, to allow her son to cope with his.

At first it is difficult to listen with an open mind; we don't realize how closed our minds are on certain subjects—especially those which have hurt us. But any kind of listening is better than continual talking. Some day, if we listen instead of talk, something someone says gets through to us and our prejudices. We then begin the long and rewarding process of learning to live with serenity and confidence.

Easy Does It

CONSIDERING THIS easy-to-believe, but hard-to-practice slogan, it would be inappropriate to hammer away at it, as all of us sometimes feel like doing in handling various Al-Anon problems.

Dealing with a new member's closed mind, for instance, can drive you frantic—you scurry around in every corner of your mind to find words that will reach that person—whereas, if you just took it easy, bided your time, someone else in your group might do an even better job.

Here, then, are thoughts of what Easy Does It (or take it easy) means to me. It means not gulping down all Twelve Steps in one undigestible lump. Some can be taken easier than others, and not necessarily in numerical order. You needn't get in a swivet if you have difficulty with the First Step—many of us do. Keep working on it. When you regress from it, recognize the fact instantly and guard against further regression. Don't brand yourself a complete failure.

If you think all your shortcomings are due to living with

an alcoholic, arrested or practicing, give consideration to taking an inventory. If the thought of taking one upsets you, wait a little. You'll do a better job on it when you know even more of the program. And be sure to do it on a day when your halo isn't hurting your head.

There's nothing brand new about the principles of the Al-Anon program. They've been around a long time; have worn well, so it isn't necessary for you to improve them; just try to live by them daily.

Easy Does It doesn't mean sitting on the small of the back with heels above the head as in the comic strips. Rather, to me at least, it means a considered appraisal of a calm, unblustering approach to daily problems; an approach that will not add fuel to a blaze but will so dampen it down as to prevent a new conflagration.

Alcoholics are volatile people to live with, and their nonalcoholic spouses are not necessarily phlegmatic. All of us can use Easy Does It. It is a reliable guidepost and all of us can benefit hugely from it.

Let Go and Let God

To ANYONE who had no difficulty with the First Step, practicing this slogan will, I believe, come easily. But if that "powerless over alcohol" bit was as difficult for you to accept as it was for me, I think you may have the same struggle with letting go.

To begin with, this slogan does not mean "Let Go and Let George Do It." Not at all. It says let God and it means God, your Higher Power, Fate, or whatever belief you live by. It means that you take a back seat and accept whatever answer is given your prayer, your request or your best efforts to keep your hands off another's life.

I never took over our family finances; I did not interfere with the relationship between my husband and my daughter; I never acted as the head of the family. My whole time was spent in trying to circumvent that first drink. I constantly besieged God with advice on how to keep my husband from it, and I supplemented this advice with practical "help" on carrying it out—like running him past a bar so he wouldn't stop off for a quickie.

I never realized the incongruity of such witless behavior. It was only when I really accepted the fact that *I* was powerless over alcohol that I could see what "Let Go and Let God" really meant: to me they are both parts of the same whole, and both have shown me just where I come in.

My husband's problem is separate and distinct from mine. I have to keep my hands off and allow him to solve it. God is infinitely wiser than I. I have seen the mess which I formerly made of our situation and which I continued to make until I learned what the First Step and Let Go and Let God was all about. I continued to make that mess in spite of all the evidence I saw in Al-Anon that the Higher Power's hands were better on the reins than mine.

When I did let go and let God, I didn't give up anything which belonged to me—I relinquished something I should never have taken over. I returned it to the proper hands and two of us benefited.

Think

AMONG THE MANY fortunate influences to which I was exposed in school, was that of Dean Flint. She was a full professor of English, a widow, and mother of two sons. Part of the creed she lived by, and you can see what a lasting impression it made on me, was that it is the business of every parent to see that the succeeding generation is better than his own.

My daughter and I have never seen eye-to-eye on this: she says human nature can't be changed. I say it has changed, and for the better. We no longer put a starving man into prison for snatching a loaf of bread; we don't kill or cripple seven and eight year old children for life by letting them work fourteen hours a day in unheated attics or basements; we no longer visit mental hospitals, seeking to be entertained by the antics of inmates. We *have* progressed. We also now recognize alcoholism as a disease, not a disgrace.

Some people still say you cannot teach old dogs new tricks. But it is my belief that man is not a dog. Not only does he have two less legs, he has an ability to think. And it is in this ability to think that he can look for help in making each succeeding generation at least a little bit better than the preceding one.

No thinking man can buy a new overcoat and hang it up beside two others, still warm and serviceable, without thinking another man is walking cold streets, shivering and uncomfortable. When he thinks of this, he gives the two away to Good Will or the Salvation Army. No thinking woman, during a milk strike, with a freezer full of food and feeding adults only, can snatch the last carton of milk from a woman with a small child.

Think! Imagine where you could be if you forgot everything as soon as it happened; if you acted always upon impulse, without considering anyone else; if you always rode off in all directions from any and all situations.

A few moments' thought can lead you to the solution of some problems; others may take hours or days. But by taking thought, sometimes by asking help of others, the proper solution can be found. And the whole world may be better off. Certainly for those living with an alcoholic, Al-Anon's thinking is priceless.

First Things First

WHAT BROUGHT YOU to Al-Anon? Help for yourself or for someone dear to you? It really doesn't matter because you soon learned that the most important thing in your life was to regain control of yourself. Living with a problem too big for you to solve alone had made inroads on your health, spirit and courage.

This, then, was the beginning. If you listened at meetings with an open mind, you learned that you needed help in regaining these qualities. You saw that others had attained all three, through following the Al-Anon program.

Especially in the beginning, this slogan "First Things First" is vitally important. If it is kept constantly in mind you will always be aware of your goals: acceptance and serenity. It will help you always to sift the important things from the unimportant; it will show you what should be done today and what can wait for tomorrow; and it will re-establish order in your life.

From spinning in a dizzying whirl over every mishap, it will show you just where to put your efforts; after all, a paper cut needs less attention than a severed artery, and "First Things First" shows you which is which, if you stop quietly to evaluate them. Gradually, with this recognition of degrees of importance, you stop that old spinning around; you gain detachment and you see where you need to put your effort.

If you came to Al-Anon for help for yourself, constant practice of determining which things come first has helped you. If you even came for help for a dear one, you may have gained it also with the calmer, more stable atmosphere you have established around you. That by-product does not always result, but you are infinitely better able to cope, once you begin to live by recognizing that certain things must and should come first, and which they are.

Words to Live By

THREE WORDS deserve to stand among our slogans: "Why Not Try?" Early in our Al-Anon days, and for many of us long before Al-Anon, when things got bad we simply gave up, went to pieces in one way or another. Thus we contributed handsomely to our own downfall. It took various parts of the program, the example of the group, and a new lease on life to prod us into attempting to overcome our indifference, our lethargy, our rejection of the world.

When I remember a much older friend of my older sister, a woman then in her middle or late sixties, it always makes me think of those who simply give up, who never consider anything but the status quo, and take it as permanent.

One icy, stormy day when Abby should never have gone out, she slipped and broke her hip in a most peculiar and dangerous way. Her doctor did all that was possible but was afraid she would never walk again. Abby asked for training in strengthening exercises and worked at them so that in three months she walked without a limp!

Then, exactly a year later, she fell again, again breaking the same hip in the same horrible way. This time the doctor was convinced she'd surely spend the rest of her life in a wheelchair. But Abby would have none of it. Again she set herself to the special exercises and again she walked. The doctor called it a miracle and it was: a miracle of determination.

Nothing but that determination to overcome a handicap helped Abby to overcome a physical catastrophe. Had she sat back and accepted the handicap, she'd still be in a wheelchair. But she determined to exhaust every possibility of help before giving up and kept trying.

There is something to help most of us in our difficulties. There is no reason for us to continue to accept them supinely. We can improve our plight, even if we cannot eliminate the cause of our distress. Why not try? We have nothing to lose and everything to gain.

Keep an Open Mind

MOST OF US have seen crabbed, soured, middle-aged or really old people, who have let life overcome them. Very often they have slitted eyes, pinched noses and straight-line mouths—gashes instead of lips. Naturally they are not attractive, receptive-looking persons. It is as difficult to get a new idea into their minds as it is to fire them with enthusiasm for the frug or the watusi.

Age is not necessarily a prerequisite to a permanently closed mind. Unfortunately, disappointment and unhappiness can lead many young persons to shut out new ideas and experiences, perhaps because some unlucky chance had thrown them back upon themselves, made them distrustful of almost everything.

To rule out all new ideas because a few proved unhelpful, or distasteful, would be as stupid as to stop eating because one had bitten into an apple, rotten at the core.

Many people come to Al-Anon in bitterness and frustration; some of the things they first hear seem incredible and unrealistic: the idea that the most fruitful place to begin work is upon one's own self is unwelcome, especially if "that old so-and-so" still drinks.

The main thing for established members, as well as newcomers, as I see it, is to give one's self every chance for mental and spiritual growth by weighing all new approaches or ideas. If we automatically rule out each offer of help, each new conception presented to us, block out each new experience, we limit ourselves to a very restricted field in which we have few opportunities to enlarge our horizons.

Each automatic rejection of a new idea makes it easier to reject the next; the habit of refusal fastens itself tight upon us. Not every new idea is right for us but we should give each due consideration.

Keeping an open mind is our way of ensuring easy accessibility to the greatest amount of help and happiness possible.

Live and Let Live

THIS SLOGAN is double-barreled. It would be well for each of us to keep both parts constantly in mind. Naturally, the first part pertains to us, personally; the second part admonishes us to allow others to live their lives.

That first "Live" should prod us into a consideration of our own lives. Are we letting never-to-return days slip by us in discontented, unhappy, aimless repudiation of what we could really accomplish if we but had the will to stir ourselves? Grant that things are about as bad as could be: our partner is still drinking; our children are getting out of hand; we are in debt; we have few friends left and we avoid them and our families as much as possible. We live practically alone, with fear and dread.

Except that my daughter never got out of hand, all those things were once true of me. And I couldn't have cared less. Sullen and sick at heart as I then was, I had so accustomed myself to indifference to the world about me that almost nothing penetrated the gloom I drew about myself.

John Donne said, "No man is an island." But I had islanded myself. It took Al-Anon, plus close association with truly wonderful Al-Anoners like Lois, Anne, Sue and Dot to stimulate me to attempt a bridge back to a more normal outlook. My early work at what we called our Clearing House further fired me with courage to return to a living life, instead of persisting in a living death. No one can really live without a compelling interest; Al-Anon became that—the focus of my new life. Thus, though tardily, I put the first "Live" into action.

The first thing to be done, if you have given up as I had, is to find some interest which will keep you from that spineless indifference to everything about you. You may be fortunate in having some talent which will give added stimulus to your Al-Anon work.

Then, just as you must have a real life for yourself, you should, in gratitude and fairness, be willing to allow others to have their lives, their opinions and their say. We all know the danger of allowing one person, no matter how wise and experienced, to dominate our groups. Not only does this prevent a free exchange of ideas, but it also prevents the spiritual growth of other members.

Sometimes it is necessary for one to learn by making a mistake. Truly wise and experienced "older members" will make every effort to allow newcomers to mature healthfully in this program by letting them live the program at their own pace; they offer what wisdom they have but don't insist on it.

Most of us would do well to keep "Live and Let Live" in the forefront of our minds, no matter how long we have been in Al-Anon.

Who Said "This Is a Selfish Program"?

FEW THINGS in our program are as confusing, to my mind, as this statement. Many people give it various interpretations. Generally speaking, I believe there must be a better word for what is meant than "selfish."

The worst interpretation I ever heard came from a woman who accepted it enthusiastically at its face value: right out in meeting she said, unblushingly, "I certainly agree this is a selfish program. If my husband dies from alcoholism, I'll have his life insurance. If he gets the AA program, he'll sober up and be able to support me. Either way, I'll be taken care of."

Selfish, according to Webster, means "Caring unduly or supremely for one's self; regarding one's own comfort, advantage, etc., in disregard or at the expense of others . . ."

Certainly no one who has really tried to live the Twelve Steps, especially in making an honest effort to "carry the message to others and to practice these principles in all our affairs," can be doing so in disregard or at the expense of others.

I believe "selfish" in this case means that the program is a *personal* one: no one can practice it for us—we must make the effort ourselves. We must look within ourselves to determine where we went wrong, and stir ourselves to make things right. We ourselves have to put the principles into practice.

Granted that we are heartily sick and tired of the mess we have made of living with an alcoholic, we may *enter* the program from the selfish motive of attaining peace within ourselves. But from the moment we actually begin to practice the Al-Anon program, I believe "selfish" changes to "personal" and we work it, not only for ourselves but for anyone else in need of help.

Discussion of "We Have No Dues or Fees"

AL-ANON is a membership organization. That is to say, members share in and determine its decisions and responsibilities. Groups, from the beginning, were polled on all matters affecting Al-Anon as a whole. Today we have delegates to the World Service Conference who accept this responsibility for their states and provinces. Groups are autonomous but concern themselves, generally, with the common good of Al-Anon rather than with their own rights and privileges.

Groups have little need of money: enough for rent, refreshments if served, and literature. Because large amounts in treasuries may cause problems, Al-Anon has never laid stress on big collections and by policy refuses contributions from outside sources.

As in AA, the secretary's usual announcement when passing the basket is, "We have no dues or fees but we do have expenses." Such a practice is fine as far as groups are concerned.

Our World Service Office, however, is a different case. It has great need of money and can look only to Al-Anon members to supply it. In little more than 15 years Al-Anon has grown from a few groups in the U.S. and Canada, to a worldwide network of some 3,600 groups. (Note: Now over 5,000)

In the 2nd quarter of 1967 alone, an average of 69 groups a month were formed and 86 proposed groups a month wrote for assistance. Nearly 25,000 FORUMS were mailed in those 3 months (over 10,000 free to groups), free Directories were sent each group; 1,386 copies of letters offering Al-Anon help were sent to institutional and prison groups. Postage alone has averaged over $900 a month all this year. (Now over $1,400 a month.)

Substantial sums, such as these figures indicate, are a bit frightening when one considers the tenuous nature of our finances, which depends primarily upon voluntary contributions of members. It frequently seems to me that we should add a bit to that oft-heard announcement: "We have no dues or fees but we do have gratitude!"

Not only do we have gratitude for what Al-Anon has done for us, we have a firm determination that it will continue to exist so that all who are yet to come may find the same help.

We cannot, in conscience, handicap our World Services Office by lack of support. That support must come from the members, far and wide, so that Al-Anon's work may not only continue as at present but expand as needed.

Discussion of the First Step

> *"We admitted we were powerless over alcohol—that our lives had become unmanageable."*

A still-popular cliché is "One must learn to walk before he can run." No one who ever watched a baby's first steps needs to be told this twice.

A few walk easily. Most put blood, sweat, toil and tears into the effort. Frustration irks them endlessly.

The more I think of Al-Anon's First Step, the more I see that it is like a baby's. It has to be taken—no progress can be made without it. But for most Al-Anons it is the most difficult.

A very few are blessed with accepting it immediately. They grasp it at once and never let go. My own daughter understood it years before I did. She was 13 when I learned and told her alcoholism was a compulsive disease which the victim could not control, once he had a drink.

Shortly thereafter things got difficult. Her father spoke sharply to her for almost the first time in her life. Afraid she'd be hurt, when we were alone I explained he'd misunderstood her or he'd never have spoken as he did.

"Don't worry," she said, matter of factly. "He'd been drinking." "What difference does that make?" I asked.

"When he's drinking he's not my father and I don't bother at all." Appalled, I said, "Drink or no drink, he is *still your father.*"

"Oh no. When he's not drinking, *he is himself and then he's my father.*"

It took me years, literally, to see she was exactly right. When an alcoholic drinks, alcohol is in control, not the alcoholic, not the person at all.

Even at that early age, my daughter saw that she herself was powerless over alcohol and that her father was too.

With this instinctive understanding of the problem, no harm ever was done to their relationship and no father and daughter ever could be closer.

Few wives or husbands attain this complete understanding easily. The drinker seems to make sense a lot of the time, though he may be talking in a blackout.

With the burden of guilt which haunts them all, the

alcoholic, when drinking, lashes out verbally at his partner, trying to equalize the responsibility.

One definition of sober is "not affected by passion or prejudice." According to this, few partners are truly sober when the other is drinking and raving.

Thus the "sober" spouse lashes back. Feelings are hurt. Misunderstandings, often serious ones, arise; harm is done. True acceptance of the fact that one is powerless over alcohol would save both heartaches and headaches.

You, as well as your partner, are powerless over alcohol. The quicker you stop trying to be an irresistible force meeting an immovable object, the quicker you will gain serenity.

The time spent concentrating your energies on trying to control another's habits and life, is that much time spent in prolonging an unmanageable situation—it's time wasted.

You are powerless over alcohol; your life, pre–Al-Anon, became unmanageable, if you're like most of us. But you're NOT powerless over yourself. Al-Anon, if you'll allow it to help you, will show you how to control yourself, to straighten out your own life.

Once you recognize alcoholism as a disease, over which both you and your partner are powerless, you have a firm base on which to build.

You do not have the disease and cannot cure it. But you do bear scars from living in turmoil. Had you understood the nature of the disease in the beginning, those scars would have been avoided.

You do, however, now have Al-Anon. You can remake your life, and yourself, if you stop this losing battle and concentrate on a way of life which will help you, your family and the alcoholic also. A tranquil home life offers everyone an inducement to do better.

There's one pre-eminent caution about this Step. Never think of it as a "once and for all time" job.

We are all too human. We all like things done our way. We must keep in mind our own limitations and our own expectations. We must allow the other person to have his.

Discussion of the Second Step

"Came to believe that a Power greater than ourselves could restore us to sanity."

People who have lived years with a practicing alcoholic mate, usually have little difficulty in acknowledging that their lives have become unmanageable. Until they understand the First Step fully, and really take it, they feel a great burden of responsibility.

They feel they have failed to understand the alcoholic; have done or not done things to help him keep sober; their love is in some way lacking or it would have prevented the excess.

Thus, and it is very understandable when they are living in such confusion, they live with a constant burden of guilt on their shoulders, a sense of having been tried and found wanting.

They have relied upon themselves too long, have tried to be supermen when they were merely mortal.

To all these weary, hopeless, desperate people, this Second Step comes as a gift straight from the blue. Many of them once had some belief, some religion, but had long since separated from it in protest. Now, after fully accepting the First Step, they are able to see what reliance upon themselves alone had done to them.

They are ready to give up their morbid sense of responsibility, are able to see that, of themselves, they can go nowhere but further down.

Into their despair comes a realization that *something*

can help them: something bigger than themselves—some call it God, some their Higher Power, some the Group Spirit and some any number of other things.

Whatever they call it, it brings release to them. By themselves, they got into a mess; this Higher Power can help them straighten it out if they cooperate.

Many have lived so long in the ruinous alcoholic atmosphere that their personalities have changed; they have deviated far from normal behavior. The changes in many cases were so gradual, or so long-established that at first it was difficult to recognize them as abnormal.

With a recognition of and dependence upon the Higher Power, however, they begin to see how far they have deteriorated. With trust in the Higher Power they set themselves to return to normality.

This Step, like so many of the others, is at once a great comfort and a greater challenge. It really separates the men from the boys to root out that stubborn resistance to the Higher Power and to cooperate with it fully.

In years of Al-Anon and AA talks, I have never heard anyone tell of calling upon God or his Higher Power in vain. Many tell of difficulty with the "spiritual angle" but come to accept and rely on it. And it works.

A Discussion of the Third Step

> "Made a decision to turn our will and our lives over to the care of God as we understood Him."

In Al-Anon, as in AA, there are no musts; the program is not religious. It is open to all. It is, however, a spiritual one and for those who believe in God this Step logically follows the first two.

Once you have acknowledged your inability to cope with things beyond your control and discovered that your own ineptness has geometrically increased your problems, you become willing to look elsewhere for help.

Those who believe in God, I have observed, seem to have an easier time accepting help. But it is not necessary to believe in Him—we have successful agnostics and atheists in Al-Anon; it just seems to take them a bit longer to get the program.

Some turn to God for help. Others call on a Higher Power, which can be anything from the group spirit to something outside of and bigger than the person himself.

I said the fortunate ones turn to God because it has always seemed to me that these people have a quiet sureness about them, an ease of acceptance, that the others slightly lack. Very possibly I am wrong. Each of us accepts all we personally can and it seems sufficient.

We come to Al-Anon with demonstrated failure behind us, with a shaken reliance upon our own judgment and management. We are looking for a way out—a way up.

Many despairing persons once had a firm belief and established communication with God. But through years of desperate loneliness, vain hope, unhappiness and ever-increasing strain, many gave up all pretense of belief. They went it alone, in a stark, bitterly miserable way.

Al-Anon's first two steps, however, showed them their record of a great deal less than success. Depending only upon themselves led them to the mess which drove them to Al-Anon to seek any way out.

By this time, those who once believed in God were ready to try anything—even going back to God—to lead them out of the morass of the unrewarding lives they were living.

Fortunately for them, it is a loving God they turned to, one who easily overlooked their lapse.

At this point they made a decision to turn their lives and their wills over to His care, each according to his understanding.

They intended to keep living up to this decision.

But having indulged themselves so long, they found it a difficult resolution to sustain.

They had spent years running everything as much their own way as they could, had come to look upon themselves as the last word in authority. Shedding such long-established habits cannot be done overnight.

They can, however, concentrate on changing themselves as fast as they are able to digest our program. If they keep an open mind, the group can show them where they go wrong, should they have a relapse.

Slowly for some, miraculously fast for others, order is restored in their lives. Courage returns. Life again becomes worth living.

(Editor's Note: As was said at the beginning, there are no musts in Al-Anon. No one has to accept any or all of the above. It is a personal interpretation, according to my own experience. Should you disagree, you should work out your own interpretation . . . there's plenty of room. It would be interesting to compare any such differences.)

Discussion of the Fourth Step

"Made a searching and fearless moral inventory of ourselves."

Anyone who takes the Al-Anon program seriously knows that conscientious, thoughtful attention must be given to each step. There is no leaping up and down the Twelve, as children do when playing games.

They were carefully planned so that each follows logically upon the preceding one. Thus, having had the courage to admit our powerlessness over alcohol, to recognize that our lives had become unmanageable, we were able to admit that help from a Power greater than ourselves was necessary to us and we became willing to let that Power help us. These first three Steps are the foundation for the fourth.

It is only after we have thoroughly studied, accepted and put the first three into practice that we are, I believe, ready for this Fourth one.

We cannot jump at it while we still believe we are responsible for our partner's excess, while we still are trying to influence or promote abstinence and are living in self-created turbulence. To be successful in this Step, we must have reached a measure of detachment, to have gained an unbiased judgment of ourselves.

This detachment, this unbiased judgment is essential because, to my way of thinking, the most important word in this Step is "fearless."

It is useless, I believe, to take an inventory if we are still wallowing in excuses: "I wouldn't do this if he/she hadn't done that." "I am sober. The mess isn't MY fault!"

It is only when we are completely ready to look conditions straight in the face, to acknowledge our part in worsening an already bad situation, that there's any value in taking it.

This takes courage enough to acknowledge to ourselves that in the past we frequently added fresh fuel to blazing scenes that were better damped down; we can say to ourselves we did it in ignorance, and with the best intentions. But we have to acknoweldge the harm we did, so that we won't continue doing it.

We also have to have enough objectivity to give ourselves credit for the things we did well. A true balance sheet always has to have two columns: a debit and a credit one.

When we can fearlessly examine our past behavior, judging only our own actions and reactions, then is the time, and not before, to my mind, to take a searching inventory.

Discussion of the Fifth Step

> "Admitted to God, to ourselves, and to another human being the exact nature of our wrongs."

The inventory Steps, Four through Ten, have a certain inescapable momentum. They also show the deepest possible understanding of human beings.

First is the fearless moral inventory, in which we seek out our weaknesses and strengths. If the inventory is really fearless and exact, it usually points the way to this Fifth Step because we cannot bear to leave things in the mess they are in.

All the Steps are progressive: admitting our wrongs to God is usually easy—most of us feel He knows them already. Admitting them to ourselves is part of the fearless inventory. The catch comes in admitting them to another human being.

I do not believe I am unique in putting the best face possible on the things I do. Unconsciously, if there are two ways to present a situation, I tend to give myself a break in choosing the less revolting one. And right there is the value of "another human being."

It is more difficult to lie to another person than to one's self; if lie is too strong a word, then the impulse to present an exact picture is stronger when another person is involved. The urge to do a wholesale job of recognizing responsibility is strengthened by the effort to make that other person understand. We can do it only by complete honesty and detachment.

Putting things into words, which must be done to make another person understand, is the most potent factor (to me) in this Step. It ensures an exact realization of wrongs done. Furthermore, that other human being has a responsibility: he or she can prevent you from going overboard in an orgy of self-recrimination; he can recognize your hits and misses if the picture you paint is a too-exaggeratedly black one.

It seems to me that one cannot take a true inventory too early in our program. One must have time to learn quite a bit about it or the inventory will not be valid. Newcomers tend to blame themselves for everything they've done, especially when a partner is still drinking. Sometimes everything they've done has been wrong but not always and not usually. They need help in recognizing where they were right—and encouragement to continue. That's where another human being can stretch out a helping hand.

If the time is right for you to take the Fourth Step, don't leave it at that. It's only one part of the next six—all equally necessary. The Fifth Step, rightly taken, lays an invaluable foundation for those to follow.

Discussion of the Sixth Step

"Were entirely ready to have God remove all these defects of character."

Two words of this Step seem to me of paramount importance: "entirely" and "all." This Step depends upon a fearless inventory and an admission to one's self, to God and to another person the exact nature of wrongs.

Granting those, comes the state of mind in which to take this Step; every one of us hates a grudging gift and that old saw, "God loves a cheerful giver," is still around. Thus we must work to ensure that we want most emphatically to be rid of these defects, that we are glad to put them behind us, ALL of them.

"All these defects" frequently reminds me of times I've determined to clean out catchalls: bits and pieces of clutter which have accumulated over the years. The day comes when I determine to toss them out in one fell swoop. But my eyes light on a yellowed letter—my first love letter! Puppy love, yes, but what a thrill it was. I've had it for years and forgotten it. Can I bear now to give it the toss? Can't I keep just this? Then I remember my resolve to put an end to all the accumulation. Out it goes.

Faults, self-indulgences, can be like that ancient letter. We've had them so long we perhaps forget they are there. But if we aim at true spiritual growth, can we give up lying and continue stealing?

Granted these last are an exaggeration, it's only a matter of degree. Can we pick and choose which defects to give up if we honestly take this Step? Thus, all means ALL and we ready ourselves for the next Step where we ask God to remove them.

Discussion of the Seventh Step

"Humbly asked Him to remove our shortcomings."

To achieve success with this Step we cannot approach it with the attitude of one asking a doctor to remove a physical defect, an ugly wart or a troublesome ingrown nail.

True, these are part of us. But they developed by themselves, from a cause unknown to us and beyond our control.

Character defects are a different thing: if we have done proper homework on the Steps preceding this one, we well know—or should—just how such defects began. We probably have spent years in the care and nurture of them; they are now so deeply entrenched in our daily lives they are difficult to uproot.

Most commonly such defects are resentment, self-pity and instant blame of another person. None of these is a desirable response to a given situation. All, in fact, stem from a lack of understanding of ourselves. With Al-Anon's guiding light we can recognize them as shortcomings within ourselves.

With this recognition and with the desire to attain the spiritual growth promised by the Al-Anon program, we can do our best to overcome these and other faults we have picked up over the troubled years.

Perhaps there are perfect human beings in the world. I have not met any in my group nor among my other friends. Depending solely upon ourselves, we run into trouble, are brought up short by failure. Thus we ask for help.

And that help is unfailing if we seek it in the right way. We should not demand it as a right, sitting back, arrogantly telling our Higher Power what to do to make us better people.

First we do our utmost to overcome our faults ourselves. Then, with full appreciation of our own shortcomings and failures, we humbly ask His help. Humility is really a sense of proportion, a yardstick of what we are worth. So it is only after we have done our best, and know it is not good enough, that we can humbly ask for help and know it will be given us.

Discussion of the Eighth Step

"Made a list of all persons we had harmed and became willing to make amends to them all."

One thing to remember when working on the Steps is that they are not just forward-going Steps: they rely heavily upon what already is past. They are like a nursemaid we had when young who never said "back and forth" as most of us do; she always went "forth and back," which is what we have to do when we begin working on a new Step.

This one is not difficult if we have a thorough-going inventory behind us. Such a review of the past shows who was hurt by our reaction to our own hurt.

A list of those persons, in black and white or graven deep in our minds, is necessary to prepare us to take the next—the Ninth Step. We have to see what wrongs we did and whether they hurt another, before we can work on becoming willing to make amends.

Frequently the greatest harm we did was to ourselves, by loss of control. We became unhappy, impatient and struck out at anyone near us because we were ourselves upset. Sometimes the other person understood and refused to be harmed by such injustice. In this case we damaged only ourselves by uncontrolled behavior.

Once we understand the damage done to ourselves, the best amends we can make is to forgive ourselves and to forget all of it, except just enough to prevent us from ever succumbing again.

Other persons, however, did not always understand what made us act as we did. Children, especially, most frequently were victims of our frustrations. They often suffered in an unhappy world of their own.

Many parents simply are unable or unwilling to admit they hurt their own children—regardless of cause. I believe this is frequently why some Al-Anon parents shy away from encouraging their children to go to Alateen. Consciously or unconsciously, they feel it would be accepting responsibility for damage done. They dismiss the whole problem by refusing to see the need for Alateen. For some people it is necessary to re-take the Fourth and Fifth Steps. For others, a comprehensive list, well pondered over, is recommended and will well repay the effort.

Becoming willing to make amends is the simplest part of this Step, I believe. Al-Anon people are not mean, vindictive creatures; they would never remain in the program were they such. So their first thought, when they realize what harm they have done, is regret for doing it and a wish to make amends. Thus they are ready to go forward to the next Step.

Discussion of the Ninth Step

"Made direct amends to such people whenever possible, except when to do so would injure them or others."

If we have earnestly, thoughtfully and prayerfully worked on the preceding eight, this Ninth Step goads us into action. We have recognized, and physically listed, those whom we have harmed. To stop there would be like breaking a leg but doing nothing about getting it set properly.

Direct amends frequently can be made: if we have harmed our families by neglect, ill-temper or harsh treatment, a change in attitude, conscientiously pursued, counterbalances the injuries. Or, if harm has come because we sloughed off work on others: refused Group, PTA or other responsibilities, on account of embarrassment or just sat back in selfish indolence, then we can make amends by accepting our full share of work in these common projects.

But many times direct amends seemingly are beyond us. For instance, the person hurt may be dead and it's too late. Or a loose tongue might have led us into intruding on someone's privacy by idle talk about a "slip" and we don't even remember the name. Also we may have completely lost touch with a person harmed, so that direct amends appear impossible.

Luckily amends still can be made in most instances because our Al-Anon responsibility is very like that of a parent: we never really requite our parents for all they have done for us but we do pay our debt to them by being the best parent possible to our children.

Our new book says, "Al-Anon responsibility is forward." That forward responsibility covers any situation where direct amends can not be made: if we have harmed one person in the past, we can help one, ten or a thousand in the present and in the future, by actively living and practicing the Al-Anon program.

Discussion of the Tenth Step

"Continued to take personal inventory and when we were wrong promptly admitted it."

Normal daily living involves constant repetition of various activities: eating, sleeping, bathing, work of all sorts and diversions to renew our spirits. Therefore it should surprise no one that living our program is not, and never will be a one-time effort.

To be successful in this program we have to take and retake most of the Twelve Steps. Human frailty erodes the best resolve to live by them unless we constantly keep aware of a tendency to relax our vigilance and to prattle, "I know the Steps—they are a wonderful way of life."

Yes, we did take a moral inventory in the Fourth Step, just as we ate breakfast this morning. But the breakfast we ate today won't carry us through tomorrow and the next day and the next. Neither will that one moral inventory.

The Tenth Step is just like breakfast. It extends the good we got from our original inventory. Because we are exposed to widely varying situations, we are also exposed to new temptations by them. We may not have to struggle with the same old faults and failures, but since we are not perfect we probably will have to struggle to shed new shortcomings.

But by the time we have come to the Tenth Step we are better armed to deal with these new defects of character. For one thing, most likely they are not as deep-seated and entrenched as previous failings, but probably they're there.

Effort put into overcoming long-established faults is a great help in uprooting new weeds in our Al-Anon gardens. But we can only rid ourselves of them if we are aware that they have sprung up.

To obtain that awareness, before the crop is well-established, we have to continue to take inventory. When wrong we must promptly admit it, but also we must encourage ourselves to keep trying, by crediting ourselves with progress made in overcoming faults . . . old and new.

This Tenth Step does not explicitly state this idea but to me it is clearly implied. There must be two sides to any balance sheet and we should assess our good points as well as our bad ones for what they are.

Discussion of the Eleventh Step

"Sought through prayer and meditation to improve our conscious contact with God as we understood Him, praying only for knowledge of His will for us and the power to carry that out."

Some of you perhaps remember the old, childish saying, when a playmate refused to do as you wished, "I'm going to pick up my dolls and go home."

I'm sure I did pick up my things on occasion and went home. But I was a child then. I have been fortunate, as an adult, not to react that way when endless "gimme" prayers seemingly brought no answer to me.

Many others were not as lucky. They write that after long years of prayer, if the situation remained unchanged, they stopped believing in God. They decided He had no interest in them; they dropped Him from their lives and it took Al-Anon to bring them back to faith.

Such an attitude by adults, seems to me today a lot like picking up your toys and going home in a pet. After all, what is the purpose of life if it is not growth? Are we to have everything our own way, exactly as we'd like it? Should we not allow others to grow and mature in theirs?

There are really only three answers to prayer: "Yes," "No," and "Wait a bit."

If our idea of God is that He is merely a source of goodies, and our responsibility to Him is to let Him give them, then it's easy to stop believing in Him when prayers repeatedly are answered with a No.

But no one can really spend much time on this Step and still cling to such a childish idea. In our own lives, with our children, we, for their best good, frequently have to deny their requests. Or we sometimes have to teach them to accept waiting for something until they are old enough to have it.

This Step helps us to the understanding that, by ourselves, we have made many mistakes. It takes a lot of faith, courage, and work on the earlier Steps to bring us to the realization that our own will has not been our best guide.

Once we accept, again or for the first time, that God is all-loving and cares for us as we do for our children, life gets easier. The closer we come to Him, the more knowledge of His will for us comes to us. With this knowledge comes the courage and power to carry it out.

Some one recently quoted a thought from an old FORUM which had been helpful. I hunted it up and found Pauline G., then WSD from Indiana, had read it somewhere and sent it in more than four years ago! It is most appropriate here!

"Many of us lose confidence in prayer because we do not realize the answer. We ask for strength and God gives us difficulties which make us strong. We pray for wisdom and God sends us problems, the solution of which develops wisdom.

"We plead for prosperity and God gives us brain and brawn with which to work. We plead for courage and God gives us dangers to overcome. We ask for favors and God gives us opportunities."

After all, if you feel you have lost contact with God, remember, Pascall says, "When you start looking for God, you have already found Him."

Discussion of the Twelfth Step

"Having had a spiritual awakening as the result of these Steps, we tried to carry this message to others, and to practice these principles in all our affairs."

You who like to take the Steps in their numerical order will find reassurance in the opening of this one. And those who prefer to jump around and perhaps skip one or two, might consider the wisdom of an orderly progression.

This Step says clearly that the spiritual awakening comes as the result of these Steps, which means the previous eleven—not two or three of them nor even six or seven; it may be worthwhile to give them more thought: to go back and make sure you have taken all of them.

Undoubtedly, if you work conscientiously on any of the Steps, you will be rewarded with a deepened spiritual awareness. But the spiritual awakening will be more complete, more lasting, if there are no blank spots in your approach to it.

Furthermore, if you have worked on all the Steps, it will be much easier for you to fulfill the second part of the Twelfth . . . that of practicing these principles in all your affairs.

Basically Al-Anon's whole program is built on the Twelfth Steps. If they are as integral a part of your consciousness as your own name and address, you will find it easier to live by them.

But if you continue, in spite of experience, to try to run your own life and that of your mate too, you'll continue to struggle in the dark, wondering why you are having so much trouble.

If you have taken the Fourth Step and let it go at that, you won't have benefited greatly. The next five need as much attention as the Fourth. And just to make sure there are no slips, there's always the Tenth Step to round out your working of the program.

There is so much satisfaction, such a sense of accomplishment, in giving a hand to someone going down for the third time, that some members rush into Twelfth Step work—that is, sharing the program with those in need of a mental or spiritual lift—as if that were the aim and entire end of this Twelfth Step.

Surely that is one part but, important as it is, it really is the topping, the strawberry jam on the peanut butter. The basic strength of Al-Anon's program comes from the spiritual awakening which results from honest work on all the preceding eleven and keeping at it.

Discussion of the First Tradition

> *"Our common welfare should come first; personal progress for the greatest number depends upon unity."*

You doubtless remember the foreword to Al-Anon's Traditions: "Group experience indicates that the unity of the Al-Anon Family Groups depends upon adherence to these Traditions."

Thus, at the start, the purpose of our Traditions is spelled out. We have the responsibility to make certain that Al-Anon's program will endure throughout the world.

The program necessarily relies upon members working for our common welfare. "If a house be divided against itself, that house cannot stand." Lincoln staked his career on this statement: "I believe this government cannot endure permanently, half slave and half free." These truths do not change.

Certainly unity is of vital importance but it still is typical of Al-Anon's broad program that there are no *musts* in the Traditions. On the contrary, they are full of *mays, shoulds, oughts* and *we needs*.

Just as the Twelve Steps provide guidance for individual members, the Twelve Traditions provide guidance to safeguard groups.

This first Tradition shows clearly that the Al-Anon fellowship is and should be, more important than any individual member. If we were split apart by a dozen different practices and interpretations of the program, there soon would be no chance for personal progress.

Therefore it should not be difficult for each of us to keep constantly aware that we are only a tiny (although important) part of a huge fellowship. We should not force personal views upon other members nor try to run our group to suit ourselves.

Each member needs his own place in the sun so that he may grow spiritually in the program. He'll never get that place if he is continually overshadowed.

Groups which regularly review the Traditions, devote time to discuss them earnestly, seldom encounter the problem of a Mr. or Mrs. Al-Anon dominating the group.

Successful groups stem from a faithful observance of this First Tradition because it engenders a spirit of unity and fair play which gives each member his opportunity to grow—at his own pace.

Discussion of the Second Tradition

> "For our group purpose there is but one authority—a loving God as He may express Himself in our group conscience. Our leaders are but trusted servants; they do not govern."

Al-Anon's program is a spiritual one, not confined to any race, creed or religious discipline. Why then is God brought directly into five of the Twelve Steps, indirectly (Power greater than ourselves which is God to some of us) into another and again into this Second Tradition?

I think the answer is because everyone believes in something. Atheists believe in their unbelief; agnostics, while not believing in an actual God, are willing to concede He might exist if it could be proved. And the rest of us have our own faiths, all quite apart from Al-Anon.

Al-Anon's Steps leave everyone free to acknowledge God "as we understood Him" and this Tradition specifies a "loving God as He may express Himself in our group conscience." Thus there is no religious difficulty about that. For unbelievers, the group conscience is the motivating force.

And think what a safeguard the group conscience is for the Al-Anon Family Groups. One member may misinterpret some part of the philosophy; one or two may go off at a tangent which some day, left unchecked, might be disrupting. This easily could happen if groups affiliated with other causes or movements.

But with the group conscience as a guide, it's difficult to see how a whole group could go wrong. The group conscience is simply an extension of that old, reliable "two heads are better than one." Thus far it has kept our fellowship hewing to the line and provided wise counsel for us all.

Lastly, this Tradition enjoins us to maintain the strict equality which exists, or should exist, in Al-Anon. We have no ruling caste; those responsible for carrying on program and group activities are there to serve the group, not to run it for personal aggrandizement.

Al-Anon's program is one for the ages. The Steps and Traditions keep it so.

Discussion of the Third Tradition

> *"The relatives of alcoholics when gathered together for mutual aid, may call themselves an Al-Anon Family Group provided that, as a group, they have no other affiliation. The only requirement for membership is that there be a problem of alcoholism in a relative or friend."*

This Third Tradition is double-barreled—both inclusive and exclusive; furthermore, it implies considerably more than it explicitly states.

To qualify for an Al-Anon Family Group, it is not enough for relatives of alcoholics to gather together. They so gather together for mutual aid and in addition they do not dissipate their efforts by diluting their primary purpose with other causes.

Groups do not meet to allow harried relatives of alcoholics to let off steam by discussion of alcoholic behavior. They meet to give aid and mutual understanding to each other, to enable members to live more peaceably and quietly with an active problem, or to help members repair the damage they have done to themselves through ignorance of the disease.

This damage frequently persists, and sometimes grows worse for a time, after the alcoholic has become sober. Too many spouses have pinned all their hopes and all their faith on the idea that the only thing needed was for the spouse to stop drinking and the millennium would begin. Sometimes it does begin with sobriety; sometimes the situation is worsened: some non-alcoholic spouses expect too much too soon; some fail to make allowance for the fact that neither party is starting fresh and rested—the alcoholic is pursued with haunting remorse and a shaky hold on a precarious and far-from-complete grasp of the AA program, while the mate is hagridden by persistent memories of endless broken promises, disappointments and distrust of continued sobriety.

If the group had another affiliation or purpose as well as Al-Anon, its efforts could be diverted and divided and fewer would be able to find any degree of serenity.

As to membership, the requirement is very explicit, ". . . problem of alcoholism in a relative or friend." Here again, more is implied: some very conscientious members occasionally question their eligibility for membership in a group if their alcoholic spouse or relatives dies.

It seems to me there is no question here whatever. They came to Al-Anon for help with an alcoholic problem; damage done by alcoholism drove them to it. They found the help they needed in the Al-Anon Group. If that need persists, even after the death of the alcoholic, it seems only logical they still are eligible to be members.

Moreover they frequently can contribute much that is valuable to the group, so that they actually give more than they receive. But even if they didn't, it seems to me they still are welcome members. Our purpose is to give help, hope and understanding to those who have suffered from problems of living with, or having lived with, alcoholism.

I believe Al-Anon's hospitable doors should always be open to anyone who comes to it for help where alcoholism is the root of one's difficulty. Death does not always end all problems nor, to me, does it end Al-Anon's responsibility for stretching out the helpful hand of fellowship.

Discussion of the Fourth Tradition

"Each group should be autonomous, except in matters affecting another group or Al-Anon or AA as a whole."

This Tradition is the simplest of the Twelve. Explicitly stated as it is, it seems difficult to believe there ever could be any misunderstanding of it. However, misunderstanding actually has arisen occasionally in the past.

One example of what almost happened, when insufficient consideration was given to plans for a public presentation of Alateen, clearly shows the vital necessity to our program of this Tradition. It further points up the scrupulous care needed to carry out the Tradition.

An overzealous sponsor, rightly proud of a remarkably fine group of youngsters, planned to present a typical meeting on television as a means of informing, impressing and interesting other teenagers living with alcoholic problems. He planned to have the participants sit in a half-circle, facing the screen!

It was only by the Grace of God that someone outside the group learned of the plan in time to call the sponsor's attention to this Fourth Tradition and to the Eleventh and Twelfth as well.

Just for a moment think of how many anonymities would have been broken had half a dozen youngsters faced that television screen! Perhaps some of the parents, AA and Al-Anon, and other relatives, would not have cared much, if at all. But many more in all likelihood would have been deeply upset.

Granted that the sponsor had planned the program, not for personal glory but to spread the word of Alateen, he definitely had given no consideration to how such a presentation would affect other Alateen groups, Al-Anon and AA.

Alcoholism for long was considered a stigma. AA, Al-Anon and Alateen work hard to get it accepted as "a disease and not a disgrace." It is little wonder that newcomers in all three fellowships are frequently greatly concerned to make their membership as little obtrusive as possible. They usually become less tense about it as time goes on but still, anonymity is the basis of the program and they have been assured theirs will be protected.

Had the sponsor given due consideration to these three all-important Traditions, he would have planned from the beginning to present the meeting as it actually was done, with the unidentified youngsters behind a screen.

We have about the widest latitude possible in our fellowships. No one wants to hedge us about with rules. But it is imperative that we safeguard everyone by giving careful thought to where our own freedom ends and that of others begins. Especially is this needful when a group considers branching out.

A large part of Al-Anon's rapid growth has stemmed from our meticulous observance of this Fourth Tradition.

Discussion of the Fifth Tradition

> "Each Al-Anon Family Group has but one purpose: to help families of alcoholics. We do this by practicing the Twelve Steps of AA ourselves, by encouraging and understanding our alcoholic relatives, and by welcoming and giving comfort to families of alcoholics."

This Tradition, like the other eleven, goes straight to the point. There is no pussyfooting, no equivocation, no detouring into side issues. It tells us decisively that Al-Anon Family Groups have only one purpose: it defines that purpose and gives definite explanations of how we can accomplish it.

First, by practicing the Twelve Steps. This is not easy to do. It was a lot simpler for us to admire them as a way of life for the alcoholic—as many of us did at first. But when we accepted them as our own way of life, when we shouldered our own responsibility for governing our lives by practicing them faithfully, we soon learned that we were abundantly rewarded for our efforts.

Second, by encouraging and understanding the alcoholic. This is even more difficult than the Steps. In fact, if I am to be honest, I find it impossible to understand more than that there is an absolute compulsion to drink after even the smallest amount of alcohol has been drunk. I don't have that compulsion; I so hate feeling the least bit ill that even contemplating the hangovers, black-outs and all the other complications of drinking too much, would scare me into letting liquor alone.

Fortunately, I believe, just understanding this much is enough. Full understanding comes from one alcoholic to another.

The best encouragement we can give alcoholics comes

from the improvement we make in ourselves and the calmer, hands-off climate we establish in our homes, through Al-Anon.

Third, by welcoming and giving comfort to families. Those of us who have found Al-Anon, with its blessed restoration of hope, courage and serenity, know that the most important thing in our lives is to keep close to Al-Anon always, so that we may share the blessings of it with others in need. All that we have learned in our fellowship, I believe, would be Dead Sea fruit if we kept it for ourselves and did not pass it on to others in need, in gratitude.

Discussion of the Sixth Tradition

> "Our Family Groups ought never to endorse, finance or lend our name to any outside enterprise, lest problems of money, property and prestige divert us from our primary spiritual aim. Although a separate entity we should always cooperate with Alcoholics Anonymous."

One of Al-Anon's greatest safeguards is explicitly stated in the opening phrases of this Tradition, with the specific reason for the admonition immediately following.

The wisdom of such a policy is very evident when you consider that the Al-Anon Family Group movement is worldwide—international in a very real sense. Al-Anon's priceless unity stems from this Tradition.

That unity would be seriously jeopardized if groups in South Dakota and South Africa spent half their time sponsoring local issues. If groups in Alberta, Australia and Argentina endorsed measures peculiar to their localities, there'd be every opportunity for politics to divide their membership. Were Al-Anon linked to any party, there'd be every chance it would lose prestige should that party fall into disrepute.

Al-Anon's primary aim, its very reason for being, is here defined as a spiritual one. You'd run into constant difficulties in keeping it spiritual if you diluted that program by mixing in worldly or material considerations particularly characteristic of your own communities. Our problem, that of learning to live with problems connected with alcoholism, is a universal one. We all do well to address our entire effort to this one subject.

The second sentence of this Tradition very properly follows the first one. We are not now, never have been and very likely never will be an integral part of Alcoholics Anonymous. The AA fellowship has enough on its own hands for it to insist that it remain separate from anything else . . . just as Al-Anon does.

Although Al-Anon is not affiliated with AA in any way, AA has cooperated with us magnificently. Without their members' help, their example and their generosity in sharing their experience, Al-Anon never could have attained such remarkable growth in so short a time.

There should be no resentment, no hurt feelings, that AA did not welcome Al-Anon into its fellowship. I do not believe any such feelings of misunderstanding now exist. AA's program is for alcoholics—Al-Anon's for living with alcoholism. We in Al-Anon are fortunate that theirs came first and they shared it so generously with us.

The debt, of each and every one of us, is great and only can be repaid by cooperating in every way we can.

Discussion of the Seventh Tradition

"Every group ought to be fully self-supporting, declining outside contributions."

Besides being the shortest of the Twelve Traditions, this one should be one of the simplest and easiest to understand. However there are frequent questions about it.

The most recent was answered in the Ask-It-Basket session of the Conference: Should tickets to an Al-Anon dance, dinner or party be sold to outsiders when a group wishes to raise money?

The answer was no, since it would jeopardize the anonymity of AA spouses, some of whom wouldn't care but others would object. Under our Tradition of cooperating with AA and guarding members' anonymity, such affairs should be kept within the fellowship.

Groups really need little money: enough to buy literature, pay rent, buy coffee and cake for meetings, support intergroups (if any), Assemblies and World Service work—those are the usual commitments. One very helpful expense that groups could undertake is to maintain a Post Office Box so that a permanent mailing address can be assured. Such a box would save both time and money at WSO in changing group records every time there is a new Secretary.

The reasoning behind this Tradition is clear, patterned as it is after AA's. It is the age-old idea that "he who pays the piper calls the tune." We could endanger our primary purpose of following Al-Anon's program, were we to accept support by government, civic organizations or philanthropists. We'd perhaps risk pressure being brought to include things other than learning to live with the problem of alcoholism.

There are times when it is tempting to accept outside bequests. So much good could be done with a gift of a thousand or more dollars, freely given. Al-Anon has always refused, although with gratitude, such legacies and gifts. Under this Tradition, Al-Anon always will refuse them and will be the stronger for it.

Discussion of the Eighth Tradition

"Al-Anon Twelfth Step work should remain forever non-professional, but our service centers may employ special workers."

One of Al-Anon's greatest safeguards is assured by this Tradition. It provides against commercialization of the program.

"Carrying the message to others" by volunteers has a thousand better chances of acceptance by a troubled person than if it were offered by professionals who make their living at it. It would be difficult to question the motive of a person who freely shares his own experience with the sole purpose of helping another.

Furthermore there is no need in Al-Anon for professional Twelfth Step workers. Part of our philosophy and our obligation in Al-Anon is to share the same enlightenment, understanding and hope we ourselves have gained from the program.

If we try to bottle it all up within ourselves, to hoard it and to forget that there are others still in darkness and despair, we reap only a fraction of Al-Anon's benefits. The program stagnates within us; we stunt our own growth. We have to share what we have gained in order to keep it.

It is in freely sharing that we strengthen our belief and our reliance on the program. We cannot idly chatter when we are intent upon making another person understand our philosophy. Rather, we have to put our minds upon just what those factors are which make the program work for us.

It is a constant re-evaluation process we use when we review our own experiences to enable us to select exactly those things we used successfully in cases like those of the persons we try to help.

It wouldn't help any spouse to be told he or she had worsened a bad situation by trying to control and manage the alcoholic's life, unless you can show what *you* did which was useless and stupid. You cannot get anyone to stop harming those about him unless *you* can show exactly what harm has been done and how.

In essence, every good Twelfth Step job involves a review, conscious or subconscious, of your own life in Al-Anon.

Since spreading the word of Al-Anon is so vital a part of the program, the second part of this Tradition is necessary. The movement began when Lois W. and Annie S. first worked with widely scattered groups of AA wives who met to practice the AA program for themselves.

There were a few established groups before 1951. Bill W. had learned of them when he made a trip across the United States and Canada to instil an interest in an AA Conference.

He returned home most enthusiastic about these groups but feared they might go their own separate ways if there weren't some central unifying office. Two volunteers, Lois and Anne B., worked seven months alone until the correspondence became too heavy. They moved their work-base to Manhattan so that others would help to lighten their load. Volunteers came—and more volunteers—and Al-Anon grew.

Very shortly, in three years or less, Al-Anon growth had so increased that volunteers could no longer handle it and the beginnings of today's fulltime staff were established. With all the world to deal with, mostly by correspondence of one kind or another, these special staff workers are now essential to maintain and foster further growth. The World Service Center could not run without them.

Intergroups find themselves in the same situation. A few loyal volunteers can supply the need in the beginning. But growth is attained at such a rapid pace in most cases that special workers must be employed.

Al-Anon, taking the lead from AA, has been wise enough to distinguish between and provide for the two kinds of Al-Anon work: Twelfth Step work, always non-professional and unpaid—clerical work, professional and paid when needed.

Discussion of the Ninth Tradition

> *"Our groups, as such, ought never be organized; but we may create service boards or committees directly responsible to those they serve."*

This Tradition is probably responsible for an ever-recurring nightmare to many jittery Al-Anon members who are apprehensive that any change, big or little, may endanger a program which has brought so much good to them. That one word, "organized," I believe, is the culprit, if a word doing the job for which it was chosen could be called a culprit.

Al-Anon, like AA, is a fellowship in which every member in every group is free to take what he likes and ignore what he doesn't. Al-Anon operates according to the

Golden Rule and our limitations are only those which keep us from hurting others or infringing upon their rights.

If it was a political organization we'd have a head, charged with keeping us in line with party policy; trying to influence our support for party office-holders and aspiring candidates for office. We'd be either majority "ins" or minority "outs," depending upon who had won the last election and was temporarily in power.

But in Al-Anon there is no power, no musts except those we make for ourselves. We do have certain leaders but their duties are limited and so is their term of office.

Our groups need Chairmen to plan and keep order at meetings; usually they are chosen for six months or at most a year. Treasurers are elected for a like period for the usual duties; some groups have Secretaries while others combine this office with that of Treasurer.

Group Representatives are essential to keep contact with Area Committees, Assemblies and to act as FORUM representatives. Where groups have special interests, such as Institutional and Public Relations work, Committee Chairmen are elected or appointed.

Our World Service Office functions as a liaison center for groups all over the world, to foster their growth and unity. It has no power to say, "This must be done." Because of its unique position as the working center for 4,500-plus groups with their wealth of experience, it is able to draw attention to and caution against certain practices which have been found to lead to trouble in the past. But it is in no way a gigantic policeman, nightstick in hand, to threaten a group's autonomy.

Nothing much but size has changed in the Al-Anon Family Groups in nearly two decades. Probably nothing ever will since we have chosen as our one authority a "loving God as He may express Himself in our group conscience."

Al-Anon constantly strives to broaden the base of those who carry on its work: the old Advisory Board was replaced nine years ago by the annual Conference of Delegates from all over the United States and Canada. We have been fortunate these past two years in having a Representative from the United Kingdom present to give us the benefit of their Al-Anon experience.

We now have a Regional Trustee from the Western United States on our Board of Trustees and look forward to another from Eastern Canada next year and a third from the Eastern U.S. the year after. They, it is hoped, will bring special experience and skills to enhance our work.

All this "creating of service boards and committees" is not organization in the political sense. Ask yourself how otherwise so much could have been done as well in so short a time?

Al-Anon has been fortunate in finding the people it needs to carry on its work as it should be carried on. With the safeguards provided in our Twelve Traditions, it seems reasonable to expect it will always be as fortunate.

Discussion of the Tenth Tradition

> "The Al-Anon Family Groups have no opinion on outside issues; hence our name ought never be drawn into public controversy."

Double-barreled shotguns are fine for giving one a quick second shot at moving objects going in different directions. But Al-Anon's ends are better served by concentrating all its ammunition toward the fixed targets of its threefold purpose.

"To welcome and give comfort to the families of alcoholics; to give understanding and encouragement to the alcoholic in the home; and to grow spiritually through living by the Twelve Steps of AA."

Even a cursory consideration of those three purposes shows they are important enough and compelling enough to stand alone—not to be mixed with diverse interests which would dilute our efforts.

Faithful practice of the Al-Anon program extends the range of every practicing member. Where he has lived with fear, distrust and despair, Al-Anon's program sets him free, not only to live his own life confidently but to give understanding assistance and strength not only to the tottering newcomer, wavering between hope and despair, but to all who need it.

There is no place in Al-Anon for official recognition of political or religious connections. Al-Anon Family Groups designedly limit their scope to handling problems caused solely by alcoholism.

As individual human beings we can, if we desire, believe that the world is flat, that eating meat is harmful, that the government should bring up all children and be responsible for everyone from the cradle to the grave. But if we involve ourselves in outside issues, we do so only as private individuals, not as Al-Anon members.

If I personally believe that astronomical expenditures for space exploration is wanton extravagance amounting practically to a swindle of public funds which could be better used to find a cure for the common cold, that is my right. But I am not free to organize an "Al-Anon Stop The Space Program Movement." I could, if anyone can imagine it, become a Carrie Nation and join a Temperance Union.

But I am not free to hitch it to our fellowship and make it an "Al-Anon Family Group Temperance Union."

Just as long as Al-Anon Family Groups remain faithful to carrying out the three avowed purposes for which they were designed, as long as they do not dissipate Al-Anon strength on divisive issues, they will continue to grow and flourish. They will continue to be the bulwark they now are for so many needful thousands around the world.

Discussion of the Eleventh Tradition

> "Our public relations policy is based on attraction rather than promotion; we need always maintain personal anonymity at the level of press, radio, TV and films. We need guard with special care the anonymity of all AA members."

This three-part Tradition demands consideration lest it become a stumbling block for the unwary. Each word is a simple one. Each point is perfectly clear. But all too often one point or another is tossed into a discussion of some proposed action as a reason for maintaining the status quo.

Take the "attraction rather than promotion" phrase. A lot of comfortable, let-George-do-it inertia can hide behind those words when an energetic, inspired Al-Anon member suggests that meeting time and place be advertised; when visits to doctors, judges, clergymen and others are proposed; or when a series of instructive newspaper articles is suggested.

Al-Anon's first purpose is to welcome and give comfort to the families of alcoholics. Nothing in this Tradition says this welcome and comfort is to be extended only by word of mouth to persons known to us. Nothing prohibits a newspaper announcement, an educational campaign to instruct the public on what Al-Anon Family Groups are.

It has always seemed to me that this situation is vividly illustrated by an old-time sailing master who needed to fill out his crew. He had two ways to do it: to list the jobs with information of pay, privileges and the benefits of life at sea. That, to me, was attraction—what we do when we try to reach those in need whom we do not know personally.

But when the captain hired press gangs to set upon drunken seamen or knock solitary wayfarers unconscious and shanghai them for forced service aboard his ship, he resorted to promotion.

Attraction, to me, is giving a choice of whether or not one eats by making food look, taste and smell appealingly or has it crammed down the throat with pumpguns as they do with Strasbourg geese when they raise them for paté de foie gras.

"At the level of press, radio, TV and films" is the motivating phrase of this Tradition. Some members are so impressed with the necessity for anonymity they overlook just why and where anonymity is good. Our Conference Approved pamphlet, "Why Is Al-Anon Anonymous?" makes a clear distinction between anonymity inside and outside the Al-Anon Family Groups.

We do not furtively slink in and out of meetings, put paper bags over our heads or issue masks to group members. Under this Tradition we speak freely, confident that nothing said in an Al-Anon meeting will be repeated outside.

Both Al-Anon and AA have benefited greatly from the press, radio, TV and films. Without their support, their generous help in bringing word of our fellowships to great masses of people, neither could have attained the growth they enjoy today. Without them, thousands upon thousands would still be suffering, searching for help.

Both Al-Anons and AAs speak freely, intimately and confidently at large meetings where these media are well represented. Their trust has never been abused when the Tradition of anonymity has been made clear to the press. It is only when a chairman has not explained the value and seriousness of guarding anonymity that some unfortunate incidents have occurred.

Our debt to Alcoholics Anonymous is so great, we'd make a poor return for all it has given us if we carelessly disregarded the third part of this Tradition which enjoins us to "guard with special care" the anonymity of all AA.

Just as we leave the drinking problem to the alcoholic, so do we leave the degree of AA anonymity to the alcoholic.

Discussion of the Twelfth Tradition

"Anonymity is the spiritual foundation of all our Traditions, ever reminding us to place principles above personalities."

Human nature never has been noted for perfection. Most of us have a great need to grow spiritually, to overcome mistakes made in the past and to learn how such mistakes can be avoided in the future.

For persons who have been adversely affected by problems of living with alcoholism, the Al-Anon Family Group program is as much of a "specific" as quinine for treating malaria. But Al-Anon's treatment is not one of pills or tablespoonfuls "to be taken every four hours." Rather it is one of helping ourselves and others by living the Al-Anon Steps and Traditions.

Entirely putting aside our obligation to protect the anonymity of our alcoholic mates, there would be little chance for spiritual growth were we to call attention to ourselves with constant reminders, broadcast at large, that we are following the Al-Anon program and that it is one of self-improvement.

If friends question a change in us because of our improved attitude, because we have finally matured a bit, have stopped being hypercritical, despondent and unduly anxious, then is the time to give credit to Al-Anon, person-to-person, not a public announcement for personal glory.

One of our greatest obligations, as well as joys, is to give hope and help to others in like circumstances who are struggling along alone. Surely our opportunities for such giving would be cut to a minimum if we seemed to present ourselves publicly as saviors of mankind, models of rectitude.

With anonymity as the spiritual base of our program, there is little danger we'll relapse into our old ways of thinking ourselves the center of the universe. We'll constantly be reminded of the hard-earned humility we have gained. We'll be glad to content ourselves with growth and let our light shine from within, rather than to bask in the limelight.

With this humility laboriously gained from self-discipline, it will be much easier for us to practice the second part of this Tradition: to place principles above personalities.

There was a time when our minds were so full of our own affairs, our disappointments, our opinions and desires, that we seldom listened to anyone; we especially ignored those who differed with us.

But Al-Anon's program, which taught us so clearly how powerless we are over many things, taught us to recognize the things we could change and those we couldn't. And it also taught us to listen. In listening, we sometimes learned that even those persons we didn't much care for, frequently had ideas worth listening to. We no longer could afford judgments on the basis of whether or not we liked or admired a person.

"Principles above personalities" is another exercise in humility and putting principles first also makes for spiritual growth.

Index of Subjects

You will find this listing of the subjects covered in our book a big help, both in planning meetings and for your personal needs.

Acceptance: 47, 83, 117, 120, 138, 154, 163, 173, 174, 183
Al-Anon: As a Fellowship: 3, 86, 121, 198
    As a Way of Life: 6, 9, 33, 37, 40, 47, 106, 140, 174, 193
    How started: 91
    Literature (Conference Approved): 147
    Purposes: 2, 19, 48, 73, 124, 161, 196
Alcoholism, A Disease: 24, 62, 63, 68, 125, 145, 196
Amends: 108
Anger: 65, 207
Changing Ourselves: 5, 29, 130
Children: 8
Detachment: 116
Discouragement: 66, 67, 122, 169, 171
Expectations: 57, 61
Faith: 31, 43, 44, 96, 190
Fear: 31, 60, 81, 82, 96, 149, 174, 175, 190, 191
Forum: 94, 95
Frustration: 82
Giving: 40, 65, 152, 153, 157
Gratitude: 112, 133
Helping the Alcoholic: 93
Hope: 31, 43, 131, 141, 152, 153
Kindness: 25, 88
Meetings: 9, 70, 89, 90, 113, 114, 115, 125, 140, 141
Open Mind: 223, 224
Patience: 76
Perfection: 28, 69, 109
Prayer: 28, 29, 34, 42, 63, 64, 127, 215
Problem Solving: 11, 80, 99, 187
Recovery in Al-Anon: 1, 31, 49, 60, 93, 191
Rejection: 22
Resentments: 35, 36, 65, 148
Self Discipline: 56
Self Esteem: 14
Self-Knowledge: 45, 46
Self-Pity: 15, 16, 165, 200, 201